The 15-Day Men's Health Book with 100+ High-Protein Recipes [4 IN 1]

The Time-Saving Plan to Raise a Leaner, Stronger, More Muscular You without Feeling Hungry

By

Giovanni Paletto

The trademarks that are used are without any consent, and the publication of the trademark is without permission or backing by the trademark owner. All trademarks and brands within this book are for clarifying purposes only and are the owned by the owners themselves, not affiliated with this document.

Table of Contents

Vegan Air Fryer Cookbook

The Healthy Air Fryer Cookbook with Pictures

Keto Air Fryer Cookbook

The 15-Day Men's Health Book of 15-Minute Workouts

Vegan Air Fryer Cookbook

Cook and Taste 50+ High-Protein Recipes. Kick start Muscles and Body Transformation, Kill Hunger and Feel More Energetic

By

Giovanni Paletto

Contents

Introduction

To have a good, satisfying life, a balanced diet is important. Tiredness and susceptibility to illnesses, many severe, arise from a lifestyle so full of junk food. Our community, sadly, does not neglect unsafe choices. People turn to immoral practices in order to satisfy desire, leading to animal torture. Two of the key explanations that people adhere to vegetarianism, a vegan-based diet that often excludes animal foods such as cheese, beef, jelly, and honey, are fitness and animal welfare.

It's essential for vegetarians to get the most nutrients out of any food, and that's where frying using an air fryer shines. The air fryer cooking will maintain as many nutrients as possible from beans and veggies, and the gadget makes it incredibly simple to cook nutritious food.

Although there are prepared vegan alternatives, the healthier choice, and far less pricey, is still to prepare your own recipes. This book provides the very first moves to being a vegan and offers 50 quick breakfast recipes, sides, snacks, and much more, so you have a solid base on which to develop.

This book will teach you all you need to thrive, whether you are either a vegan and only need more meal choices or have just begun contemplating transforming your diet.

What is Cooking Vegan?

In recent decades, vegetarianism has become quite common, as individuals understand just how toxic the eating patterns of civilization have become. We are a society that enjoys meat, and, unfortunately, we go to dishonest measures to get the food we like. More citizens are choosing to give up beef and, unlike vegans, other livestock items due to various health issues, ethical issues, or both. Their diet moves to one focused on plants, whole grains, beans, fruit, seeds, nuts, and vegan varieties of the common dish.

What advantages would veganism have?

There are a lot of advantages to a diet away from all animal items. Only a few includes:

- Healthier hair, skin, and nails

- High energy

- Fewer chances of flu and cold

- Fewer migraines

- Increased tolerance to cancer

- Strengthened fitness of the heart

Although research has proven that veganism will contribute to reducing BMI, it must not be followed for the mere sake of weight reduction. "Vegan" does not indicate "lower-calorie," and if you wish to reduce weight, other healthier activities, including exercising and consuming water, can complement the diet.

Air Fryer

A common kitchen gadget used to create fried foods such as beef, baked goods and potato chips is an air fryer. It provides a crunchy, crisp coating by blowing hot air across the food. This also leads to a chemical reaction commonly known as the Maillard effect, which happens in the presence of heat in between reducing sugar and amino acid. This adds to shifts in food color and taste. Due to the reduced amount of calories and fat, air-fried items are marketed as a healthier substitute to deep-fried foods.

Rather than fully soaking the food in fat, air-frying utilizes just a teaspoon to create a flavor and feel equivalent to deep-fried foods.

The flavor and appearance of the fried food in the air are similar to the deep fryer outcomes: On the surface, crispy; from the inside, soft. You do need to use a limited amount of oil, though, or any at all (based on what you're baking). But indeed, contrary to deep frying, if you agree to use only 1-2 teaspoons of plant-based oil with spices and you stuck to air-frying vegetables rather than anything else, air frying is certainly a better option.

The secret to weight loss, decreased likelihood of cardiovascular illness and better long-term wellbeing as we mature is any gadget that assists you and your friends in your vegetarian game.

Air fryer's Working Process:

The air fryer is a worktop kitchen gadget that operates in the same manner as a traditional oven. To become acquainted with the operating theory of the traditional oven, you will need a little study. The air fryer uses rotating hot air to fry and crisp your meal, close to the convection oven. In a traditional convection oven, the airflow relies on revolving fans, which blast hot air around to produce an even or equalized temperature dispersal throughout the oven.

This is compared to the upward airflow of standard ovens, where the warm place is typically the oven's tip. And although the air fryer is not quite like the convection oven, it is a great approximation of it in the field of airflow for most components. The gadget has an air inlet at the top that lets air in and a hot air outlet at the side. All of these features are used to monitor the temperature within the air fryer. Temperatures will rise to 230 ° C, based on the sort of air fryer you're buying.

In conjunction with any grease, this hot air is used for cooking the food in the bowl within the device, if you like. Yes, if you want a taste of the oil, you should apply more oil. To jazz up the taste of the meal, simply add a little more to the blend. But the key concept behind the air fryer is to reduce the consumption of calories and fat without reducing the amount of taste.

Using air frying rather than deep frying saves between 70-80 calories, according to researchers. The growing success of recipes for air fryers is simply attributed to its impressive performance. It is simple to use and less time-consuming than conventional ovens.

This is more or less a lottery win for people searching for healthy alternative to deep-frying, as demonstrated by its widespread popularity in many homes today.

In contrast to conventional ovens or deep frying, the air fryer creates crispy, crunchy, wonderful, and far fewer fatty foods in less duration. For certain individuals like us; this is what distinguishes air fryer recipes.

Tips for using an Air Fryer

1. The food is cooked easily. Air fried, unlike conventional cooking techniques, cut the cooking time a great deal. Therefore, to stop burning the food or getting a not-so-great flavor, it is best to hold a close eye on the gadget. Notice, remember that the smaller the food on the basket, the shorter the cooking period, which implies that the food cooks quicker.

2. You may need to reduce the temperature at first. Bear in mind that air fryers depend on the flow of hot air, which heats up rapidly. This ensures that it's better, to begin with, a low temperature so that the food cooks equally. It is likely that when the inside is already cooking, the exterior of the food is all cooked and begins to become dark or too dry.

3. When air fryers are in operation, they create some noise. If you are new to recipes for air fryers, you may have to realize that air fryers create noise while working. When it's in service, a whirring tone emanates from the device. However, the slight annoyance pales in contrast to the various advantages of having an air fryer.

4. Hold the grate within the container at all hours. As previously mentioned, the air fryer has a container inside it, where the food is put and permitted to cook. This helps hot air to flow freely around the food, allowing for even cooking.

5. Don't stuff the air fryer with so much food at once. If you plan to make a meal for one guy, with only one batch, you would most definitely be able to get your cooking right. If you're cooking for two or more individuals, you can need to plan

the food in groups. With a 4 - 5 quart air fryer, you can always need to cook in groups, depending on the size and sort of air fryer you have. This not only means that your device works longer but also keeps your food from cooking unevenly. You shouldn't have to turn the air fryer off as you pull out the basket since it simply turns off on its own until the basket is out. Often, make sure the drawer is completely retracted; otherwise, the fryer would not turn back on.

6. Take the basket out of the mix and mix the ingredients. You might need to move the food around or switch it over once every few minutes, based on the dish you're preparing and the time it takes to prepare your dinner.

The explanation for this is that even cooking can be done. Certain recipes involve the foods in the basket to shake and shuffle throughout the cooking phase. And an easy-to-understand checklist is given for each recipe to direct you thru the cycle.

7. The air fryer does not need cooking mist. It isn't needed. In order to prevent the urge to use non-stick frying spray in the container, you must deliberately take care of this. The basket is now coated with a non-stick covering, so what you need to do is fill your meal inside the container and push it back in.

Outcome

You can create nutritious meals very simply and fast, right in the comfort of your house. There are many excellent recipes for producing healthier meals and nutritious foods, which you can notice in the air fryer recipes illustrated in this book. However, you'll need to pay careful attention to the ingredients and know-how to easily use the air fryer to do this. To get straightforward guidance on installation and usage, you can need to refer to the company's manual.

CHAPTER 1: Breakfast Recipes

1. Toasted French toast

Preparation time: 2 minutes

Cooking time: 5 minutes

Servings: 1 people

Ingredients:

- ½ Cup of Unsweetened Shredded Coconut

- 1 Tsp. Baking Powder

- ½ Cup Lite Culinary Coconut Milk

- 2 Slices of Gluten-Free Bread (use your favorite)

Directions:

1. Stir together the baking powder and coconut milk in a large rimmed pot.

2. On a tray, layout your ground coconut.

3. Pick each loaf of your bread and dip it in your coconut milk for the very first time, and then pass it to the ground coconut, let it sit for a few minutes, then cover the slice entirely with the coconut.

4. Place the covered bread loaves in your air fryer, cover it, adjust the temperature to about 350 ° F and set the clock for around 4 minutes.

5. Take out from your air fryer until done, and finish with some maple syrup of your choice. French toast is done. Enjoy!

2. Vegan Casserole

Preparation time: 10-12 minutes

Cooking time: 15-20 minutes

Servings: 2-3 people

Ingredients:

- 1/2 cup of cooked quinoa

- 1 tbsp. of lemon juice

- 2 tbsp. of water

- 2 tbsp. of plain soy yogurt

- 2 tbsp. of nutritional yeast

- 7 ounces of extra-firm tofu about half a block, drained but not pressed

- 1/2 tsp. of ground cumin

- 1/2 tsp. of red pepper flakes

- 1/2 tsp. of freeze-dried dill

- 1/2 tsp. of black pepper

- 1/2 tsp. of salt

- 1 tsp. of dried oregano

- 1/2 cup of diced shiitake mushrooms

- 1/2 cup of diced bell pepper I used a combination of red and green

- 2 small celery stalks chopped

- 1 large carrot chopped

- 1 tsp. of minced garlic

- 1 small onion diced

- 1 tsp. of olive oil

Directions:

1. Warm the olive oil over medium-low heat in a big skillet. Add your onion and garlic and simmer till the onion is transparent (for about 3 to 6 minutes). Add your bell pepper, carrot, and celery and simmer for another 3 minutes.

Mix the oregano, mushrooms, pepper, salt, cumin, dill, and red pepper powder. Mix completely and lower the heat to low. If the vegetables tend to cling, stir regularly and add in about a teaspoon of water.

2. Pulse the nutritional yeast, tofu, water, yogurt, and some lemon juice in a food mixer until fluffy. To your skillet, add your tofu mixture. Add in half a cup of cooked quinoa. Mix thoroughly.

3. Move to a microwave-proof plate or tray that works for your air fryer basket.

4. Cook for around 15 minutes at about 350°F (or 18 to 20 minutes at about 330°F, till it turns golden brown).

5. Please take out your plate or tray from your air fryer and let it rest for at least five minutes before eating.

3. Vegan Omelet

Preparation time: 15 minutes

Cooking time: 16 minutes

Servings: 3 people

Ingredients:

- ½ cup of grated vegan cheese

- 1 tbsp. of water

- 1 tbsp. of brags

- 3 tbsp. of nutritional yeast

- ¼ tsp. of basil

- ¼ tsp. of garlic powder

- ¼ tsp. of onion powder

- ¼ tsp. of pepper

- ½ tsp. of cumin

- ½ tsp. of turmeric

- ¼ tsp. of salt

- ¼ cup of chickpea flour (or you may use any bean flour)

- ½ cup of finely diced veggies (like chard, kale, dried mushrooms, spinach, watermelon radish etc.)

- half a piece of tofu (organic high in protein kind)

Directions:

4. Blend all your ingredients in a food blender or mixer, excluding the vegetables and cheese.

5. Move the batter from the blender to a container and combine the vegetables and cheese in it. Since it's faster, you could use both hands to combine it.

6. Brush the base of your air fryer bucket with some oil.

7. Put a couple of parchment papers on your counter. On the top of your parchment paper, place a cookie cutter of your desire.

8. In your cookie cutter, push 1/6 of the paste. Then raise and put the cookie cutter on a different section of your parchment paper.

9. Redo the process till you have about 6 pieces using the remainder of the paste.

10. Put 2 or 3 of your omelets at the base of your air fryer container. Using some oil, brush the topsides of the omelets.

11. Cook for around 5 minutes at about 370 °, turn and bake for another 4 minutes or more if needed. And redo with the omelets that remain.

12. Offer with sriracha mayo or whatever kind of dipping sauce you prefer. Or use them for a sandwich at breakfast.

4. Waffles with Vegan chicken

Preparation time: 10 minutes

Cooking time: 15 minutes

Servings: 2 people

Ingredients:

Fried Vegan Chicken:

- ¼ to ½ teaspoon of Black Pepper

- ½ teaspoon of Paprika

- ½ teaspoon of Onion Powder

- ½ teaspoon of Garlic Powder

- 2 teaspoon of Dried Parsley

- 2 Cups of Gluten-Free Panko

- ¼ Cup of Cornstarch

- 1 Cup of Unsweetened Non-Dairy Milk

- 1 Small Head of Cauliflower

Yummy Cornmeal Waffles:

- ½ teaspoon of Pure Vanilla Extract

- ¼ Cup of Unsweetened Applesauce

- ½ Cup of Unsweetened Non-Dairy Milk

- 1 to 2 TB Erythritol (or preferred sweetener)

- 1 teaspoon Baking Powder

- ¼ Cup of Stoneground Cornmeal

- ⅔ Cup of Gluten-Free All-Purpose Flour

Toppings:

- Vegan Butter

- Hot Sauce

- Pure Maple Syrup

Directions:

For making your Vegan Fried Chicken:

1. Dice the cauliflower (you wouldn't have to be careful in this) into big florets and put it aside.

2. Mix the cornstarch and milk in a tiny pot.

3. Throw the herbs, panko, and spices together in a big bowl or dish.

4. In the thick milk mixture, soak your cauliflower florets, then cover the soaked bits in the prepared panko mix before putting the wrapped floret into your air fryer bucket.

5. For the remaining of your cauliflower, redo the same process.

6. Set your air fryer clock for around 15 minutes to about 400 ° F and let the cauliflower air fry.

For making you're Waffles:

1. Oil a regular waffle iron and warm it up.

2. Mix all your dry ingredients in a pot, and then blend in your wet ingredients until you have a thick mixture.

3. To create a big waffle, utilize ½ of the mixture and redo the process to create another waffle for a maximum of two persons.

To Organize:

1. Put on dishes your waffles, place each with ½ of the cooked cauliflower, now drizzle with the hot sauce, syrup, and any extra toppings that you want. Serve warm!

5. Tempeh Bacon

Preparation time: 15 minutes plus 2 hour marinating time

Cooking time: 10 minutes

Servings: 4 people

Ingredients:

- ½ teaspoon of freshly grated black pepper

- ½ teaspoon of onion powder

- ½ teaspoon of garlic powder

- 1 ½ teaspoon of smoked paprika

- 1 teaspoon of apple cider vinegar

- 1 tablespoon of olive oil (plus some more for oiling your air fryer)

- 3 tablespoon of pure maple syrup

- ¼ cup of gluten-free, reduced-sodium tamari

- 8 oz. of gluten-free tempeh

Directions:

1. Break your Tempeh cube into two parts and boil for about 10 minutes, some more if required. To the rice cooker bowl, add a cup of warm water. Then, put the pieces of tempeh into the steamer basket of the unit. Close the cover, push the button for heat or steam cooking (based on your rice cooker's type or brand), and adjust the steaming timer for around 10 minutes.

2. Let the tempeh cool completely before taking it out of the rice cooker or your steamer basket for around 5 minutes.

3. Now make the sauce while cooking the tempeh. In a 9" x 13" baking tray, incorporate all the rest of your ingredients and mix them using a fork. Then set it aside and ready the tempeh.

4. Put the tempeh steamed before and cooled on a chopping board, and slice into strips around 1/4' wide. Put each slice gently in the sauce. Then roll over each slice gently. Seal and put in the fridge for two to three hours or even overnight, rotating once or twice during the time.

5. Turn the bits gently one more time until you are about to create the tempeh bacon. And if you would like, you may spoon over any leftover sauce.

6. Put your crisper plate/tray into the air fryer if yours came with one instead of a built-in one. Oil the base of your crisper tray or your air fryer basket slightly with some olive oil or using an olive oil spray that is anti-aerosol.

7. Put the tempeh slices in a thin layer gently in your air fryer bucket. If you have a tiny air fryer, you will have to air fry it in two or multiple rounds. Air fry for around 10-15 minutes at about 325 ° F before the slices are lightly

golden but not burnt. You may detach your air fryer container to inspect it and make sure it's not burnt. It normally takes about 10 minutes.

6. Delicious Potato Pancakes

Preparation time: 5 minutes

Cooking time: 15 minutes

Servings: 4 people

Ingredients:

- black pepper according to taste

- 3 tablespoon of flour

- ¼ teaspoon of pepper

- ¼ teaspoon of salt

- ½ teaspoon of garlic powder

- 2 tablespoon of unsalted butter

- ¼ cup of milk

- 1 beaten egg

- 1 medium onion, chopped

Directions:

1. Preheat the fryer to about 390° F and combine the potatoes, garlic powder, eggs, milk, onion, pepper, butter, and salt in a small bowl; add in the flour and make a batter.

2. Shape around 1/4 cup of your batter into a cake.

3. In the fryer's cooking basket, put the cakes and cook for a couple of minutes.

4. Serve and enjoy your treat!

CHAPTER 2: Air Fryer Main Dishes

1. Mushroom 'n Bell Pepper Pizza

Preparation time: 5 minutes

Cooking time: 10 minutes

Servings: 10 people

Ingredients:

- salt and pepper according to taste

- 2 tbsp. of parsley

- 1 vegan pizza dough

- 1 shallot, chopped

- 1 cup of oyster mushrooms, chopped

- ¼ red bell pepper, chopped

Directions:

1. Preheat your air fryer to about 400°F.

2. Cut the pie dough into small squares. Just set them aside.

3. Put your bell pepper, shallot, oyster mushroom, and parsley all together into a mixing dish.

4. According to taste, sprinkle with some pepper and salt.

5. On top of your pizza cubes, put your topping.

6. Put your pizza cubes into your air fryer and cook for about 10 minutes.

2. Veggies Stuffed Eggplants

Preparation time: 5 minutes

Cooking time: 14 minutes

Servings: 5 people

Ingredients:

- 2 tbsp. of tomato paste

- Salt and ground black pepper, as required

- ½ tsp. of garlic, chopped

- 1 tbsp. of vegetable oil

- 1 tbsp. of fresh lime juice

- ½ green bell pepper, seeded and chopped

- ¼ cup of cottage cheese, chopped

- 1 tomato, chopped

- 1 onion, chopped

- 10 small eggplants, halved lengthwise

Directions:

1. Preheat your air fryer to about 320°F and oil the container of your air fryer.

2. Cut a strip longitudinally from all sides of your eggplant and scrape out the pulp in a medium-sized bowl.

3. Add lime juice on top of your eggplants and place them in the container of your Air Fryer.

4. Cook for around a couple of minutes and extract from your Air Fryer.

5. Heat the vegetable oil on medium-high heat in a pan and add the onion and garlic.

6. Sauté for around 2 minutes and mix in the tomato, salt, eggplant flesh, and black pepper.

7. Sauté and add bell pepper, tomato paste, cheese, and cilantro for roughly 3 minutes.

8. Cook for around a minute and put this paste into your eggplants.

9. Shut each eggplant with its lids and adjust the Air Fryer to 360°F.

10. Organize and bake for around 5 minutes in your Air Fryer Basket.

11. Dish out on a serving tray and eat hot.

3. Air-fried Falafel

Preparation time: 10 minutes

Cooking time: 25 minutes

Servings: 6 people

Ingredients:

- Salt and black pepper according to taste

- 1 teaspoon of chili powder

- 2 teaspoon of ground coriander

- 2 teaspoon of ground cumin

- 1 onion, chopped

- 4 garlic cloves, chopped

- Juice of 1 lemon

- 1 cup of fresh parsley, chopped

- ½ cup of chickpea flour

Directions:

1. Add flour, coriander, chickpeas, lemon juice, parsley, onion, garlic, chili, cumin, salt, turmeric, and pepper to a processor and mix until mixed, not too battery; several chunks should be present.

2. Morph the paste into spheres and hand-press them to ensure that they are still around.

3. Spray using some spray oil and place them in a paper-lined air fryer bucket; if necessary, perform in groups.

4. Cook for about 14 minutes at around 360°F, rotating once mid-way through the cooking process.

5. They must be light brown and crispy.

4. Almond Flour Battered Wings

Preparation time: 10 minutes

Cooking time: 25 minutes

Servings: 4 people

Ingredients:

- Salt and pepper according to taste

- 4 tbsp. of minced garlic

- 2 tbsp. of stevia powder

- 16 pieces of vegan chicken wings

- ¾ cup of almond flour

- ¼ cup of butter, melted

Directions:

1. Preheat your air fryer for about 5 minutes.

2. Mix the stevia powder, almond flour, vegan chicken wings, and garlic in a mixing dish. According to taste, sprinkle with some black pepper and salt.

3. Please put it in the bucket of your air fryer and cook at about 400°F for around 25 minutes.

4. Ensure you give your fryer container a shake midway through the cooking process.

5. Put in a serving dish after cooking and add some melted butter on top. Toss it to coat it completely.

5. Spicy Tofu

Preparation time: 5 minutes

Cooking time: 13 minutes

Servings: 3 people

Ingredients:

- Salt and black pepper, according to taste

- 1 tsp. of garlic powder

- 1 tsp. of onion powder

- 1½ tsp. of paprika

- 1½ tbsp. of avocado oil

- 3 tsp. of cornstarch

- 1 (14-ounces) block extra-firm tofu, pressed and cut into ¾-inch cubes

Directions:

1. Preheat your air fryer to about 390°F and oil the container of your air fryer with some spray oil.

2. In a medium-sized bowl, blend the cornstarch, oil, tofu, and spices and mix to cover properly.

3. In the Air Fryer basket, place the tofu bits and cook for around a minute, flipping twice between the cooking times.

4. On a serving dish, spread out the tofu and enjoy it warm.

6. Sautéed Bacon with Spinach

Preparation time: 5 minutes

Cooking time: 9 minutes

Servings: 2 people

Ingredients:

- 1 garlic clove, minced

- 2 tbsp. of olive oil

- 4-ounce of fresh spinach

- 1 onion, chopped

- 3 meatless bacon slices, chopped

Directions:

1. Preheat your air fryer at about 340° F and oil the air fryer's tray with some olive oil or cooking oil spray.

2. In the Air Fryer basket, put garlic and olive oil.

3. Cook and add in the onions and bacon for around 2 minutes.

4. Cook and mix in the spinach for approximately 3 minutes.

5. Cook for 4 more minutes and plate out in a bowl to eat.

7. Garden Fresh Veggie Medley

Preparation time: 5 minutes

Cooking time: 15 minutes

Servings: 4 people

Ingredients:

- 1 tbsp. of balsamic vinegar

- 1 tbsp. of olive oil

- 2 tbsp. of herbs de Provence

- 2 garlic cloves, minced

- 2 small onions, chopped

- 3 tomatoes, chopped

- 1 zucchini, chopped

- 1 eggplant, chopped

- 2 yellow bell peppers seeded and chopped

- Salt and black pepper, according to taste.

Directions:

1. Preheat your air fryer at about 355° F and oil up the air fryer basket.

2. In a medium-sized bowl, add all the ingredients and toss to cover completely.

3. Move to the basket of your Air Fryer and cook for around 15 minutes.

4. After completing the cooking time, let it sit in the air fryer for around 5 minutes and plate out to serve warm.

8. Colorful Vegetable Croquettes

Preparation time: 5 minutes

Cooking time: 10 minutes

Servings: 4 people

Ingredients:

- 1/2 cup of parmesan cheese, grated

- 2 eggs

- 1/4 cup of coconut flour

- 1/2 cup of almond flour

- 2 tbsp. of olive oil

- 3 tbsp. of scallions, minced

- 1 clove garlic, minced

- 1 bell pepper, chopped

- 1/2 cup of mushrooms, chopped

- 1/2 tsp. of cayenne pepper

- Salt and black pepper, according to taste.

- 2 tbsp. of butter

- 4 tbsp. of milk

- 1/2 pound of broccoli

Directions:

1. Boil your broccoli in a medium-sized saucepan for up to around 20 minutes. With butter, milk, black pepper, salt, and cayenne pepper, rinse the broccoli and mash it.

2. Add in the bell pepper, mushrooms, garlic, scallions, and olive oil and blend properly. Form into patties with the blend.

3. Put the flour in a deep bowl; beat your eggs in a second bowl; then put the parmesan cheese in another bowl.

4. Dip each patty into your flour, accompanied by the eggs and lastly the parmesan cheese, push to hold the shape.

5. Cook for around 16 minutes, turning midway through the cooking period, in the preheated Air Fryer at about 370° F. Bon appétit!

9. Cheesy Mushrooms

Preparation time: 3 minutes

Cooking time: 8 minutes

Servings: 4 people

Ingredients:

- 1 tsp. of dried dill

- 2 tbsp. of Italian dried mixed herbs

- 2 tbsp. of olive oil

- 2 tbsp. of cheddar cheese, grated

- 2 tbsp. of mozzarella cheese, grated

- Salt and freshly ground black pepper, according to taste

- 6-ounce of button mushrooms stemmed

Directions:

Preheat the air fryer at around 355° F and oil your air fryer basket.

In a mixing bowl, combine the Italian dried mixed herbs, mushrooms, salt, oil, and black pepper and mix well to cover.

In the Air Fryer bucket, place the mushrooms and cover them with some cheddar cheese and mozzarella cheese.

To eat, cook for around 8 minutes and scatter with dried dill.

10. Greek-style Roasted Vegetables

Preparation time: 10 minutes

Cooking time: 25 minutes

Servings: 3 people

Ingredients:

- 1/2 cup of Kalamata olives, pitted

- 1 (28-ounce) canned diced tomatoes with juice

- 1/2 tsp. of dried basil

- Sea salt and freshly cracked black pepper, according to taste

- 1 tsp. of dried rosemary

- 1 cup of dry white wine

- 2 tbsp. of extra-virgin olive oil

- 2 bell peppers, cut into 1-inch chunks

- 1 red onion, sliced

- 1/2 pound of zucchini, cut into 1-inch chunks

- 1/2 pound of cauliflower, cut into 1-inch florets

- 1/2 pound of butternut squash, peeled and cut into 1-inch chunks

Directions:

1. Add some rosemary, wine, olive oil, black pepper, salt, and basil along with your vegetables toss until well-seasoned.

2. Onto a lightly oiled baking dish, add 1/2 of the canned chopped tomatoes; scatter to fill the base of your baking dish.

3. Add in the vegetables and add the leftover chopped tomatoes to the top. On top of tomatoes, spread the Kalamata olives.

4. Bake for around 20 minutes at about 390° F in the preheated Air Fryer, turning the dish midway through your cooking cycle. Serve it hot and enjoy it!

11. Vegetable Kabobs with Simple Peanut Sauce

Preparation time: 10 minutes

Cooking time: 30 minutes

Servings: 4 people

Ingredients:

- 1/3 tsp. of granulated garlic

- 1 tsp. of dried rosemary, crushed

- 1 tsp. of red pepper flakes, crushed

- Sea salt and ground black pepper, according to your taste.

- 2 tbsp. of extra-virgin olive oil

- 8 small button mushrooms, cleaned

- 8 pearl onions, halved

- 2 bell peppers, diced into 1-inch pieces

- 8 whole baby potatoes, diced into 1-inch pieces

Peanut Sauce:

- 1/2 tsp. of garlic salt

- 1 tbsp. of soy sauce

- 1 tbsp. of balsamic vinegar

- 2 tbsp. of peanut butter

Directions:

1. For a few minutes, dunk the wooden chopsticks in water.

2. String the vegetables onto your chopsticks; drip some olive oil all over your chopsticks with the vegetables on it; dust with seasoning.

3. Cook for about 1 minute at 400°F in the preheated Air Fryer.

Peanut Sauce:

1. In the meantime, mix the balsamic vinegar with some peanut butter, garlic salt and some soy sauce in a tiny dish. Offer the kabobs with a side of peanut sauce. Eat warm!

12. Hungarian Mushroom Pilaf

Preparation time: 10 minutes

Cooking time: 50 minutes

Servings: 4 people

Ingredients:

- 1 tsp. of sweet Hungarian paprika

- 1/2 tsp. of dried tarragon

- 1 tsp. of dried thyme

- 1/4 cup of dry vermouth

- 1 onion, chopped

- 2 garlic cloves

- 2 tbsp. of olive oil

- 1 pound of fresh porcini mushrooms, sliced

- 2 tbsp. of olive oil

- 3 cups of vegetable broth

- 1 ½ cups of white rice

Directions:

1. In a wide saucepan, put the broth and rice, add some water, and bring it to a boil.

2. Cover with a lid and turn the flame down to a low temperature and proceed to cook for the next 18 minutes or so. After cooking, let it rest for 5 to 10 minutes, and then set aside.

3. Finally, in a lightly oiled baking dish, mix the heated, fully cooked rice with the rest of your ingredients.

4. Cook at about 200° degrees for around 20 minutes in the preheated Air Fryer, regularly monitoring to even cook.

5. In small bowls, serve. Bon appétit!

13. Chinese cabbage Bake

Preparation time: 15 minutes

Cooking time: 35 minutes

Servings: 4 people

Ingredients:

- 1 cup of Monterey Jack cheese, shredded

- 1/2 tsp. of cayenne pepper

- 1 cup of cream cheese

- 1/2 cup of milk

- 4 tbsp. of flaxseed meal

- 1/2 stick butter

- 2 garlic cloves, sliced

- 1 onion, thickly sliced

- 1 jalapeno pepper, seeded and sliced

- Sea salt and freshly ground black pepper, according to taste.

- 2 bell peppers, seeded and sliced

- 1/2 pound of Chinese cabbage, roughly chopped

Directions:

1. Heat the salted water in a pan and carry it to a boil. For around 2 to 3 minutes, steam the Chinese cabbage. To end the cooking process, switch the Chinese cabbage to cold water immediately.

2. Put your Chinese cabbage in a lightly oiled casserole dish. Add in the garlic, onion, and peppers.

3. Next, over low fire, melt some butter in a skillet. Add in your flaxseed meal steadily and cook for around 2 minutes to create a paste.

4. Add in the milk gently, constantly whisking until it creates a dense mixture. Add in your cream cheese. Sprinkle some cayenne pepper, salt, and black pepper. To the casserole tray, transfer your mixture.

5. Cover with some Monterey Jack cheese and cook for about 2 minutes at around 390° F in your preheated Air Fryer. Serve it warm.

14. Brussels sprouts With Balsamic Oil

Preparation time: 5 minutes

Cooking time: 15 minutes

Servings: 4 people

Ingredients:

- 2 tbsp. of olive oil

- 2 cups of Brussels sprouts, halved

- 1 tbsp. of balsamic vinegar

- ¼ tsp. of salt

Directions:

1. For 5 minutes, preheat your air fryer.

2. In a mixing bowl, blend all of your ingredients to ensure the zucchini fries are very well coated. Put the fries in the basket of an air fryer.

3. Close it and cook it at about 350°F for around 15 minutes.

15. Aromatic Baked Potatoes with Chives

Preparation time: 15 minutes

Cooking time: 45 minutes

Servings: 2 people

Ingredients:

- 2 tbsp. of chives, chopped

- 2 garlic cloves, minced

- 1 tbsp. of sea salt

- 1/4 tsp. of smoked paprika

- 1/4 tsp. of red pepper flakes

- 2 tbsp. of olive oil

- 4 medium baking potatoes, peeled

Directions:

1. Toss the potatoes with your seasoning, olive oil, and garlic.

2. Please put them in the basket of your Air Fryer. Cook at about 400° F for around 40 minutes just until the potatoes are fork soft in your preheated Air Fryer.

3. Add in some fresh minced chives to garnish. Bon appétit!

16.Easy Vegan "chicken"

Preparation time: 10 minutes

Cooking time: 20 minutes

Servings: 4 people

Ingredients:

- 1 tsp. of celery seeds

- 1/2 tsp. of mustard powder

- 1 tsp. of cayenne pepper

- 1/4 cup of all-purpose flour

- 1/2 cup of cornmeal

- 8 ounces of soy chunks

- Sea salt and ground black pepper, according to taste.

Directions:

1. In a skillet over medium-high flame, cook the soya chunks in plenty of water. Turn off the flame and allow soaking for several minutes. Drain the remaining water, wash, and strain it out.

2. In a mixing bowl, combine the rest of the components. Roll your soy chunks over the breading paste, pressing lightly to stick.

3. In the slightly oiled Air Fryer basket, place your soy chunks.

4. Cook at about 390° for around 10 minutes in your preheated Air Fryer, rotating them over midway through the cooking process; operate in batches if required. Bon appétit!

17. Paprika Vegetable Kebab's

Preparation time: 10 minutes

Cooking time: 20 minutes

Servings: 4 people

Ingredients:

- 1/2 tsp. of ground black pepper

- 1 tsp. of sea salt flakes

- 1 tsp. of smoked paprika

- 1/4 cup of sesame oil

- 2 tbsp. of dry white wine

- 1 red onion, cut into wedges

- 2 cloves garlic, pressed

- 1 tsp. of whole grain mustard

- 1 fennel bulb, diced

- 1 parsnip, cut into thick slices

- 1 celery, cut into thick slices

Directions:

1. Toss all of the above ingredients together in a mixing bowl to uniformly coat. Thread the vegetables alternately onto the wooden skewers.

2. Cook for around 15 minutes at about 380° F on your Air Fryer grill plate.

3. Turn them over midway during the cooking process.

4. Taste, change the seasonings if needed and serve steaming hot.

18. Spiced Soy Curls

Preparation time: 5 minutes

Cooking time: 10 minutes

Servings: 2 people

Ingredients:

- 1 tsp. of poultry seasoning

- 2 tsp. of Cajun seasoning

- ¼ cup of fine ground cornmeal

- ¼ cup of nutritional yeast

- 4 ounces of soy curls

- 3 cups of boiling water

- Salt and ground white pepper, as needed

Directions:

1. Dip the soy curls for around a minute or so in hot water in a heat-resistant tub.

2. Drain your soy coils using a strainer and force the excess moisture out using a broad spoon.

3. Mix the cornmeal, nutritional yeast, salt, seasonings, and white pepper well in a mixing bowl.

4. Transfer your soy curls to the bowl and coat well with the blend. Let the air-fryer temperature to about 380° F. Oil the basket of your air fryers.

5. Adjust soy curls in a uniform layer in the lined air fryer basket. Cook for about 10 minutes in the air fryer, turning midway through the cycle.

6. Take out the soy curls from your air fryer and put them on a serving dish. Serve it steaming hot.

19. Cauliflower & Egg Rice Casserole

Preparation time: 5 minutes

Cooking time: 15 minutes

Servings: 4 people

Ingredients:

- 2 eggs, beaten

- 1 tablespoon of soy sauce

- Salt and black pepper according to taste.

- ½ cup of chopped onion

- 1 cup of okra, chopped

- 1 yellow bell pepper, chopped

- 2 teaspoon of olive oil

Directions:

1. Preheat your air fryer to about 380° F. Oil a baking tray with spray oil. Pulse the cauliflower till it becomes like thin rice-like capsules in your food blender.

2. Now add your cauliflower rice to a baking tray mix in the okra, bell pepper, salt, soy sauce, onion, and pepper and combine well.

3. Drizzle a little olive oil on top along with the beaten eggs. Put the tray in your air fryer and cook for about a minute. Serve it hot.

20. Hollandaise Topped Grilled Asparagus

Preparation time: 2 minutes

Cooking time: 15 minutes

Servings: 6 people

Ingredients:

- A punch of ground white pepper

- A pinch of mustard powder

- 3 pounds of asparagus spears, trimmed

- 3 egg yolks

- 2 tbsp. of olive oil

- 1 tsp. of chopped tarragon leaves

- ½ tsp. of salt

- ½ lemon juice

- ½ cup of butter, melted

- ¼ tsp. of black pepper

Directions:

1. Preheat your air fryer to about 330° F. In your air fryer, put the grill pan attachment.

2. Mix the olive oil, salt, asparagus, and pepper into a Ziploc bag. To mix all, give everything a quick shake. Load onto the grill plate and cook for about 15 minutes.

3. In the meantime, beat the lemon juice, egg yolks, and salt in a double boiler over a moderate flame until velvety.

4. Add in the melted butter, mustard powder, and some white pepper. Continue whisking till the mixture is creamy and thick. Serve with tarragon leaves as a garnish.

5. Pour the sauce over the asparagus spears and toss to blend.

21. Crispy Asparagus Dipped In Paprika-garlic Spice

Preparation time: 2 minutes

Cooking time: 15 minutes

Servings: 5 people

Ingredients:

- ¼ cup of almond flour

- ½ tsp. of garlic powder

- ½ tsp. of smoked paprika

- 10 medium asparagus, trimmed

- 2 large eggs, beaten

- 2 tbsp. of parsley, chopped

- Salt and pepper according to your taste

Directions:

1. For about 5 minutes, preheat your air fryer.

2. Mix the almond flour, garlic powder, parsley, and smoked paprika in a mixing dish. To taste, season with some salt and black pepper.

3. Soak your asparagus in the beaten eggs, and then dredge it in a combination of almond flour.

4. Put in the bowl of your air fryer. Close the lid. At about 350°F, cook for around a minute.

22. Eggplant Gratin with Mozzarella Crust

Preparation time: 10 minutes

Cooking time: 30 minutes

Servings: 2 people

Ingredients:

- 1 tablespoon of breadcrumbs

- ¼ cup of grated mozzarella cheese

- Cooking spray

- Salt and pepper according to your taste

- ¼ teaspoon of dried marjoram

- ¼ teaspoon of dried basil

- 1 teaspoon of capers

- 1 tablespoon of sliced pimiento-stuffed olives

- 1 clove garlic, minced

- ⅓ cup of chopped tomatoes

- ¼ cup of chopped onion

- ¼ cup of chopped green pepper

- ¼ cup of chopped red pepper

Directions:

1. Put the green pepper, eggplant, onion, red pepper, olives, tomatoes, basil marjoram, garlic, salt, capers, and pepper in a container and preheat your air fryer to about 300° F.

2. Lightly oil a baking tray with a spray of cooking olive oil.

3. Fill your baking with the eggplant combination and line it with the vessel.

4. Place some mozzarella cheese on top of it and top with some breadcrumbs. Put the dish in the frying pan and cook for a few minutes.

23. Asian-style Cauliflower

Preparation time: 10 minutes

Cooking time: 25 minutes

Servings: 4 people

Ingredients:

- 2 tbsp. of sesame seeds

- 1/4 cup of lime juice

- 1 tbsp. of fresh parsley, finely chopped

- 1 tbsp. of ginger, freshly grated

- 2 cloves of garlic, peeled and pressed

- 1 tbsp. of sake

- 1 tbsp. of tamari sauce

- 1 tbsp. of sesame oil

- 1 onion, peeled and finely chopped

- 2 cups of cauliflower, grated

Directions:

1. In a mixing bowl, mix your onion, cauliflower, tamari sauce, sesame oil, garlic, sake, and ginger; whisk until all is well integrated.

2. Air-fry it for around a minute at about 400° F.

3. Pause your Air Fryer. Add in some parsley and lemon juice.

4. Cook for an extra 10 minutes at about 300° degrees F in the air fryer.

5. In the meantime, in a non-stick pan, toast your sesame seeds; swirl them continuously over medium-low heat. Serve hot on top of the cauliflower with a pinch of salt and pepper.

24. Two-cheese Vegetable Frittata

Preparation time: 15 minutes

Cooking time: 35 minutes

Servings: 2 people

Ingredients:

- ⅓ cup of crumbled Feta cheese

- ⅓ cup of grated Cheddar cheese

- Salt and pepper according to taste

- ⅓ cup of milk

- 4 eggs, cracked into a bowl

- 2 teaspoon of olive oil

- ¼ lb. of asparagus, trimmed and sliced thinly

- ¼ cup of chopped chives

- 1 small red onion, sliced

- 1 large zucchini, sliced with a 1-inch thickness

- ⅓ cup of sliced mushrooms

Directions:

1. Preheat your air fryer to about 380° F. Set aside your baking dish lined with some parchment paper. Put salt, milk, and pepper into the egg bowl; whisk evenly.

2. Put a skillet on the stovetop over a moderate flame, and heat your olive oil. Add in the zucchini, asparagus, baby spinach, onion, and mushrooms; stir-fry for around 5 minutes. Transfer the vegetables into your baking tray, and finish with the beaten egg.

3. Put the tray into your air fryer and finish with cheddar and feta cheese.

4. For about 15 minutes, cook. Take out your baking tray and add in some fresh chives to garnish.

25. Rice & Beans Stuffed Bell Peppers

Preparation time: 10 minutes

Cooking time: 15 minutes

Servings: 5 people

Ingredients:

- 1 tbsp. of Parmesan cheese, grated

- ½ cup of mozzarella cheese, shredded

- 5 large bell peppers, tops removed and seeded

- 1½ tsp. of Italian seasoning

- 1 cup of cooked rice

- 1 (15-ounces) can of red kidney beans, rinsed and drained

- 1 (15-ounces) can of diced tomatoes with juice

- ½ small bell pepper, seeded and chopped

Directions:

1. Combine the tomatoes with juice, bell pepper, rice, beans, and Italian seasoning in a mixing dish. Using the rice mixture, fill each bell pepper uniformly.

2. Preheat the air fryer to 300° F. Oil the basket of your air fryer with some spray oil. Put the bell peppers in a uniform layer in your air fryer basket.

3. Cook for around 12 minutes in the air fryer. In the meantime, combine the Parmesan and mozzarella cheese in a mixing dish.

4. Remove the peppers from the air fryer basket and top each with some cheese mix. Cook for another 3 -4 minutes in the air fryer

5. Take the bell peppers from the air fryer and put them on a serving dish. Enable to cool slowly before serving. Serve it hot.

26. Parsley-loaded Mushrooms

Preparation time: 5 minutes

Cooking time: 15 minutes

Servings: 2 people

Ingredients:

- 2 tablespoon of parsley, finely chopped

- 2 teaspoon of olive oil

- 1 garlic clove, crushed

- 2 slices white bread

- salt and black pepper according to your taste

Directions:

1. Preheat the air fryer to about 360° F. Crush your bread into crumbs in a food blender. Add the parsley, garlic, and pepper; blend with the olive oil and mix.

2. Remove the stalks from the mushrooms and stuff the caps with breadcrumbs. In your air fryer basket, position the mushroom heads. Cook for a few minutes, just until golden brown and crispy.

27. Cheesy Vegetable Quesadilla

Preparation time: 2 minutes

Cooking time: 15 minutes

Servings: 1 people

Ingredients:

- 1 teaspoon of olive oil

- 1 tablespoon of cilantro, chopped

- ½ green onion, sliced

- ¼ zucchini, sliced

- ¼ yellow bell pepper, sliced

- ¼ cup of shredded gouda cheese

Directions:

1. Preheat your air fryer to about 390° F. Oil a basket of air fryers with some cooking oil.

2. Put a flour tortilla in your air fryer basket and cover it with some bell pepper, Gouda cheese, cilantro, zucchini, and green onion. Take the other tortilla to cover and spray with some olive oil.

3. Cook until slightly golden brown, for around 10 minutes. Cut into 4 slices for serving when ready. Enjoy!

28. Creamy 'n Cheese Broccoli Bake

Preparation time: 10 minutes

Cooking time: 30 minutes

Servings: 2 people

Ingredients:

- 1/4 cup of water

- 1-1/2 teaspoons of butter, or to taste

- 1/2 cup of cubed sharp Cheddar cheese

- 1/2 (14 ounces) can evaporate milk, divided

- 1/2 large onion, coarsely diced

- 1 tbsp. of dry bread crumbs, or to taste

- salt according to taste

- 2 tbsp. of all-purpose flour

- 1-pound of fresh broccoli, coarsely diced

Directions:

1. Lightly oil the air-fryer baking pan with cooking oil. Add half of the milk and flour into a pan and simmer at about 360° F for around 5 minutes.

2. Mix well midway through the cooking period. Remove the broccoli and the extra milk. Cook for the next 5 minutes after fully blending.

3. Mix in the cheese until it is fully melted. Mix the butter and bread crumbs well in a shallow tub. Sprinkle the broccoli on top.

4. At about 360° F, cook for around 20 minutes until the tops are finely golden brown. Enjoy and serve warm.

29. Sweet & Spicy Parsnips

Preparation time: 12 minutes

Cooking time: 44 minutes

Servings: 6 people

Ingredients:

- ¼ tsp. of red pepper flakes, crushed

- 1 tbsp. of dried parsley flakes, crushed

- 2 tbsp. of honey

- 1 tbsp. of n butter, melted

- 2 pounds of a parsnip, peeled and cut into 1-inch chunks

- Salt and ground black pepper, according to your taste.

Directions:

1. Let the air-fryer temperature to about 355° F. Oil the basket of your air fryers. Combine the butter and parsnips in a big dish.

2. Transfer the parsnip pieces into the lined air fryer basket arranges them in a uniform layer. Cook for a few minutes in the fryer.

3. In the meantime, combine the leftover ingredients in a large mixing bowl.

4. Move the parsnips into the honey mixture bowl after around 40 minutes and toss them to coat properly.

5. Again, in a uniform layer, organize the parsnip chunks into your air fryer basket.

6. Air-fry for another 3-4 minutes. Take the parsnip pieces from the air fryer and pass them onto the serving dish. Serve it warm.

30. Zucchini with Mediterranean Dill Sauce

Preparation time: 20 minutes

Cooking time: 60 minutes

Servings: 4 people

Ingredients:

- 1/2 tsp. of freshly cracked black peppercorns

- 2 sprigs thyme, leaves only, crushed

- 1 sprig rosemary, leaves only, crushed

- 1 tsp. of sea salt flakes

- 2 tbsp. of melted butter

- 1 pound of zucchini, peeled and cubed

For your Mediterranean Dipping:

- 1 tbsp. of olive oil

- 1 tbsp. of fresh dill, chopped

- 1/3 cup of yogurt

- 1/2 cup of mascarpone cheese

Directions:

1. To start, preheat your Air Fryer to 350° F. Now, add ice cold water to the container with your potato cubes and let them sit in the bath for about 35 minutes.

2. Dry your potato cubes with a hand towel after that. Whisk together the sea salt flakes, melted butter, thyme, rosemary, and freshly crushed peppercorns in a mixing container. This butter/spice mixture can be rubbed onto the potato cubes.

3. In the cooking basket of your air fryer, air-fry your potato cubes for around 18 to 20 minutes or until cooked completely; ensure you shake the potatoes at least once during cooking to cook them uniformly.

4. In the meantime, by mixing the rest of the ingredients, create the Mediterranean dipping sauce. To dip and eat, serve warm potatoes with Mediterranean sauce!

31. Zesty Broccoli

Preparation time: 10 minutes

Cooking time: 15 minutes

Servings: 4 people

Ingredients:

- 1 tbsp. of butter

- 1 large crown broccoli, chopped into bite-sized pieces

- 1 tbsp. of white sesame seeds

- 2 tbsp. of vegetable stock

- ½ tsp. of red pepper flakes, crushed

- 3 garlic cloves, minced

- ½ tsp. of fresh lemon zest, grated finely

- 1 tbsp. of pure lemon juice

Directions:

1. Preheat the Air fryer to about 355° F and oil an Air fryer pan with cooking spray. In the Air fryer plate, combine the vegetable stock, butter, and lemon juice.

2. Move the mixture and cook for about 2 minutes into your Air Fryer. Cook for a minute after incorporating the broccoli and garlic.

3. Cook for a minute with lemon zest, sesame seeds, and red pepper flakes. Remove the dish from the oven and eat immediately.

32. Chewy Glazed Parsnips

Preparation time: 15 minutes

Cooking time: 44 minutes

Servings: 6 people

Ingredients:

- ¼ tsp. of red pepper flakes, crushed

- 1 tbsp. of dried parsley flakes, crushed

- 2 tbsp. of maple syrup

- 1 tbsp. of butter, melted

- 2 pounds of parsnips, skinned and chopped into 1-inch chunks

Directions:

1. Preheat the Air fryer to about 355° F and oil your air fryer basket. In a wide mixing bowl, combine the butter and parsnips and toss well to cover. Cook for around 40 minutes with the parsnips in the Air fryer basket.

2. In the meantime, combine in a wide bowl the rest of your ingredients. Move this mix to your basket of the air fryer and cook for another 4 minutes or so. Remove the dish from the oven and eat promptly.

33. Hoisin-glazed Bok Choy

Preparation time: 5 minutes

Cooking time: 10 minutes

Servings: 4 people

Ingredients:

- 1 tbsp. of all-purpose flour

- 2 tbsp. of sesame oil

- 2 tbsp. of hoisin sauce

- 1/2 tsp. of sage

- 1 tsp. of onion powder

- 2 garlic cloves, minced

- 1 pound of baby Bok choy, roots removed, leaves separated

Directions:

1. In a lightly oiled Air Fryer basket, put the onion powder, garlic, Bok Choy, and sage. Cook for around 3 minutes at about 350° F in a preheated Air Fryer.

2. Whisk together the sesame oil, hoisin sauce, and flour in a deep mixing dish. Drizzle over the Bok choy with the gravy. Cook for an extra minute. Bon appétit!

34. Green Beans with Okra

Preparation time: 10 minutes

Cooking time: 20 minutes

Servings: 2 people

Ingredients:

- 3 tbsp. of balsamic vinegar

- ¼ cup of nutritional yeast

- ½ (10-ounces) of bag chilled cut green beans

- ½ (10-ounces) of bag chilled cut okra

- Salt and black pepper, according to your taste.

Directions:

1. Preheat your Air fryer to about 400° F and oil the air fryer basket.

2. In a wide mixing bowl, toss together the salt, green beans, okra, vinegar, nutritional yeast, and black pepper.

3. Cook for around 20 minutes with the okra mixture in your Air fryer basket. Dish out into a serving plate and eat warm.

35. Celeriac with some Greek Yogurt Dip

Preparation time: 12 minutes

Cooking time: 25 minutes

Servings: 2 people

Ingredients:

- 1/2 tsp. of sea salt

- 1/2 tsp. of ground black pepper, to taste

- 1 tbsp. of sesame oil

- 1 red onion, chopped into 1 1/2-inch piece

- 1/2 pound of celeriac, chopped into 1 1/2-inch piece

Spiced Yogurt:

- 1/2 tsp. of chili powder

- 1/2 tsp. of mustard seeds

- 2 tbsp. of mayonnaise

- 1/4 cup of Greek yogurt

Directions:

1. In the slightly oiled cooking basket, put the veggies in one uniform layer. Pour sesame oil over the veggies.

2. Season with a pinch of black pepper and a pinch of salt. Cook for around 20 minutes at about 300° F, tossing the basket midway through your cooking cycle.

3. In the meantime, whisk all the leftover ingredients into the sauce. Spoon the sauce over the veggies that have been cooked. Bon appétit!

36. Wine & Garlic Flavored Vegetables

Preparation time: 7-10 minutes

Cooking time: 15 minutes

Servings: 4 people

Ingredients:

- 4 cloves of garlic, minced

- 3 tbsp. of red wine vinegar

- 1/3 cup of olive oil

- 1 red onion, diced

- 1 package frozen diced vegetables

- 1 cup of baby Portobello mushrooms, diced

- 1 tsp. of Dijon mustard

- 1 ½ tbsp. of honey

- Salt and pepper according to your taste

- ¼ cup of chopped fresh basil

Directions:

1. Preheat the air fryer to about 330° F. In the air fryer, put the grill pan attachment.

2. Combine the veggies and season with pepper, salt, and garlic in a Ziploc container. To mix all, give everything a strong shake. Dump and cook for around 15 minutes on the grill pan.

3. Additionally, add the remainder of the ingredients into a mixing bowl and season with some more salt and pepper. Drizzle the sauce over your grilled vegetables.

37.Spicy Braised Vegetables

Preparation time: 10 minutes

Cooking time: 25 minutes

Servings: 4 people

Ingredients:

- 1/2 cup of tomato puree
- 1/4 tsp. of ground black pepper
- 1/2 tsp. of fine sea salt
- 1 tbsp. of garlic powder
- 1/2 tsp. of fennel seeds
- 1/4 tsp. of mustard powder
- 1/2 tsp. of porcini powder
- 1/4 cup of olive oil
- 1 celery stalk, chopped into matchsticks

- 2 bell peppers, deveined and thinly diced

- 1 Serrano pepper, deveined and thinly diced

- 1 large-sized zucchini, diced

Directions:

1. In your Air Fryer cooking basket, put your peppers, zucchini, sweet potatoes, and carrot.

2. Drizzle with some olive oil and toss to cover completely; cook for around 15 minutes in a preheated Air Fryer at about 350°F.

3. Make the sauce as the vegetables are frying by quickly whisking the remaining ingredients (except the tomato ketchup). Slightly oil up a baking dish that fits your fryer.

4. Add the cooked vegetables to the baking dish, along with the sauce, and toss well to cover.

5. Turn the Air Fryer to about 390° F and cook for 2-4 more minutes with the vegetables. Bon appétit!

CHAPTER 3: Air Fryer Snack Side Dishes and Appetizer Recipes

1. Crispy 'n Tasty Spring Rolls

Preparation time: 5 minutes

Cooking time: 15 minutes

Servings: 4 people

Ingredients:

- 8 spring roll wrappers

- 1 tsp. of nutritional yeast

- 1 tsp. of corn starch + 2 tablespoon water

- 1 tsp. of coconut sugar

- 1 tbsp. of soy sauce

- 1 medium carrot, shredded

- 1 cup of shiitake mushroom, sliced thinly

- 1 celery stalk, chopped

- ½ tsp. of ginger, finely chopped

Directions:

1. Mix your carrots, celery stalk, soy sauce, coconut sugar, ginger, and nutritional yeast with each other in a mixing dish.

2. Have a tbsp. of your vegetable mix and put it in the middle of your spring roll wrappers.

3. Roll up and secure the sides of your wraps with some cornstarch.

4. Cook for about 15 minutes or till your spring roll wraps is crisp in a preheated air fryer at 200F.

2. Spinach & Feta Crescent Triangles

Preparation time: 10 minutes

Cooking time: 20 minutes

Servings: 4 people

Ingredients:

- ¼ teaspoon of salt

- 1 teaspoon of chopped oregano

- ¼ teaspoon of garlic powder

- 1 cup of crumbled feta cheese

- 1 cup of steamed spinach

Directions:

1. Preheat your air fryer to about 350 F, and then roll up the dough over a level surface that is gently floured.

2. In a medium-sized bowl, mix the spinach, feta, salt, oregano, and ground garlic cloves. Split your dough into four equal chunks.

3. Split the mix of feta/spinach among the four chunks of dough. Fold and seal your dough using a fork.

4. Please put it on a baking tray covered with parchment paper, and then put it in your air fryer.

5. Cook until nicely golden, for around 1 minute.

3. Healthy Avocado Fries

Preparation time: 5 minutes

Cooking time: 20 minutes

Servings: 2 people

Ingredients:

- ¼ cup of aquafaba

- 1 avocado, cubed

- Salt as required

Directions:

1. Mix the aquafaba, crumbs, and salt in a mixing bowl.

2. Preheat your air fryer to about 390°F and cover the avocado pieces uniformly in the crumbs blend.

3. Put the ready pieces in the cooking bucket of your air fryer and cook for several minutes.

4. Twice-fried Cauliflower Tater Tots

Preparation time: 5 minutes

Cooking time: 16 minutes

Servings: 12 people

Ingredients:

- 3 tbsp. Of oats flaxseed meal + 3 tbsp. of water)

- 1-pound of cauliflower, steamed and chopped

- 1 tsp. of parsley, chopped

- 1 tsp. of oregano, chopped

- 1 tsp. of garlic, minced

- 1 tsp. of chives, chopped

- 1 onion, chopped

- 1 flax egg (1 tablespoon 3 tablespoon desiccated coconuts)

- ½ cup of nutritional yeast

- salt and pepper according to taste

- ½ cup of bread crumbs

Directions:

1. Preheat your air fryer to about 390 degrees F.

2. To extract extra moisture, place the steamed cauliflower onto a ring and a paper towel.

3. Put and mix the remainder of your ingredients, excluding your bread crumbs, in a small mixing container.

4. Use your palms, blend it until well mixed and shapes into a small ball.

5. Roll your tater tots over your bread crumbs and put them in the bucket of your air fryer.

6. For a minute, bake. Raise the cooking level to about 400 F and cook for the next 10 minutes.

5. Cheesy Mushroom & Cauliflower Balls

Preparation time: 10 minutes

Cooking time: 50 minutes

Servings: 4 people

Ingredients:

- Salt and pepper according to taste

- 2 sprigs chopped fresh thyme

- ¼ cup of coconut oil

- 1 cup of Grana Padano cheese

- 1 cup of breadcrumbs

- 2 tablespoon of vegetable stock

- 3 cups of cauliflower, chopped

- 3 cloves garlic, minced

- 1 small red onion, chopped

- 3 tablespoon of olive oil

Directions:

1. Over moderate flame, put a pan. Add some balsamic vinegar. When the oil is heated, stir-fry your onion and garlic till they become transparent.

2. Add in the mushrooms and cauliflower and stir-fry for about 5 minutes. Add in your stock, add thyme and cook till your cauliflower has consumed the stock. Add pepper, Grana Padano cheese, and salt.

3. Let the mix cool down and form bite-size spheres of your paste. To harden, put it in the fridge for about 30 minutes.

4. Preheat your air fryer to about 350°F.

5. Add your coconut oil and breadcrumbs into a small bowl and blend properly.

6. Take out your mushroom balls from the fridge, swirl the breadcrumb paste once more, and drop the balls into your breadcrumb paste.

7. Avoid overcrowding, put your balls into your air fryer's container and cook for about 15 minutes, flipping after every 5 minutes to ensure even cooking.

8. Serve with some tomato sauce and brown sugar.

6. Italian Seasoned Easy Pasta Chips

Preparation time: 5 minutes

Cooking time: 10 minutes

Servings: 2 people

Ingredients:

- 2 cups of whole wheat bowtie pasta

- 1 tbsp. of olive oil

- 1 tbsp. of nutritional yeast

- 1 ½ tsp. of Italian seasoning blend

- ½ tsp. of salt

Directions:

1. Put the accessory for the baking tray into your air fryer.

2. Mix all the ingredients in a medium-sized bowl, offer it a gentle stir.

3. Add the mixture to your air fryer basket.

4. Close your air fryer and cook at around 400°degrees F for about 10 minutes.

7. Thai Sweet Potato Balls

Preparation time: 10 minutes

Cooking time: 50 minutes

Servings: 4 people

Ingredients:

- 1 cup of coconut flakes

- 1 tsp. of baking powder

- 1/2 cup of almond meal

- 1/4 tsp. of ground cloves

- 1/2 tsp. of ground cinnamon

- 2 tsp. of orange zest

- 1 tbsp. of orange juice

- 1 cup of brown sugar

- 1 pound of sweet potatoes

Directions:

1. Bake your sweet potatoes for around 25 to 30 minutes at about 380° F till they become soft; peel and mash them in a medium-sized bowl.

2. Add orange zest, orange juice, brown sugar, ground cinnamon, almond meal, cloves, and baking powder. Now blend completely.

3. Roll the balls around in some coconut flakes.

4. Bake for around 15 minutes or until fully fried and crunchy in the preheated Air Fryer at about 360° F.

5. For the rest of the ingredients, redo the same procedure. Bon appétit!

8. Barbecue Roasted Almonds

Preparation time: 5 minutes

Cooking time: 20 minutes

Servings: 6 people

Ingredients:

- 1 tbsp. of olive oil

- 1/4 tsp. of smoked paprika

- 1/2 tsp. of cumin powder

- 1/4 tsp. of mustard powder

- 1/4 tsp. of garlic powder

- Sea salt and ground black pepper, according to taste

- 1 ½ cups of raw almonds

Directions:

1. In a mixing pot, mix all your ingredients.

2. Line the container of your Air Fryer with some baking parchment paper. Arrange the covered almonds out in the basket of your air fryer in a uniform layer.

3. Roast for around 8 to 9 minutes at about 340°F, tossing the bucket once or twice. If required, work in groups.

4. Enjoy!

9. Croissant Rolls

Preparation time: 2 minutes

Cooking time: 6 minutes

Servings: 8 people

Ingredients:

- 4 tbsp. of butter, melted

- 1 (8-ounces) can croissant rolls

Directions:

1. Adjust the air-fryer temperature to about 320°F. Oil the basket of your air fryers.

2. Into your air fryer basket, place your prepared croissant rolls.

3. Airs fry them for around 4 minutes or so.

4. Flip to the opposite side and cook for another 2-3 minutes.

5. Take out from your air fryer and move to a tray.

6. Glaze with some melted butter and eat warm.

10. Curry' n Coriander Spiced Bread Rolls

Preparation time: 5 minutes

Cooking time: 15 minutes

Servings: 5 people

Ingredients:

- salt and pepper according to taste

- 5 large potatoes, boiled

- 2 sprigs, curry leaves

- 2 small onions, chopped

- 2 green chilies, seeded and chopped

- 1 tbsp. of olive oil

- 1 bunch of coriander, chopped

- ½ tsp. of turmeric

- 8 slices of vegan wheat bread, brown sides discarded

- ½ tsp. of mustard seeds

Directions:

1. Mash your potatoes in a bowl and sprinkle some black pepper and salt according to taste. Now set aside.

2. In a pan, warm up the olive oil over medium-low heat and add some mustard seeds. Mix until the seeds start to sputter.

3. Now add in the onions and cook till they become transparent. Mix in the curry leaves and turmeric powder.

4. Keep on cooking till it becomes fragrant for a couple of minutes. Take it off the flame and add the mixture to the potatoes.

5. Mix in the green chilies and some coriander. This is meant to be the filling.

6. Wet your bread and drain excess moisture. In the center of the loaf, put a tbsp. of the potato filling and gently roll the bread so that the potato filling is fully enclosed within the bread.

7. Brush with some oil and put them inside your air fryer basket.

8. Cook for around 15 minutes in a preheated air fryer at about 400°F.

9. Ensure that the air fryer basket is shaken softly midway through the cooking period for an even cooking cycle.

11. Scrumptiously Healthy Chips

Preparation time: 5 minutes

Cooking time: 10 minutes

Servings: 2 people

Ingredients:

- 2 tbsp. of olive oil

- 2 tbsp. of almond flour

- 1 tsp. of garlic powder

- 1 bunch kale

- Salt and pepper according to taste

Directions:

1. For around 5 minutes, preheat your air fryer.

2. In a mixing bowl, add all your ingredients, add the kale leaves at the end and toss to completely cover them.

3. Put in the basket of your fryer and cook until crispy for around 10 minutes.

12. Kid-friendly Vegetable Fritters

Preparation time: 5 minutes

Cooking time: 20 minutes

Servings: 4 people

Ingredients:

- 2 tbsp. of olive oil

- 1/2 cup of cornmeal

- 1/2 cup of all-purpose flour

- 1/2 tsp. of ground cumin

- 1 tsp. of turmeric powder

- 2 garlic cloves, pressed

- 1 carrot, grated

- 1 sweet pepper, seeded and chopped

- 1 yellow onion, finely chopped

- 1 tbsp. of ground flaxseeds

- Salt and ground black pepper, according to taste

- 1 pound of broccoli florets

Directions:

1. In salted boiling water, blanch your broccoli until al dente, for around 3 to 5 minutes. Drain the excess water and move to a mixing bowl; add in the rest of your ingredients to mash the broccoli florets.

2. Shape the paste into patties and position them in the slightly oiled Air Fryer basket.

3. Cook for around 6 minutes at about 400° F, flipping them over midway through the cooking process; if needed, operate in batches.

4. Serve hot with some Vegenaise of your choice. Enjoy it!

13. Avocado Fries

Preparation time: 10 minutes

Cooking time: 50 minutes

Servings: 4 people

Ingredients:

- 2 avocados, cut into wedges

- 1/2 cup of parmesan cheese, grated

- 2 eggs

- Sea salt and ground black pepper, according to taste.

- 1/2 cup of almond meal

- 1/2 head garlic (6-7 cloves)

Sauce:

- 1 tsp. of mustard

- 1 tsp. of lemon juice

- 1/2 cup of mayonnaise

Directions:

1. On a piece of aluminum foil, put your garlic cloves and spray some cooking spray on it. Wrap your garlic cloves in the foil.

2. Cook for around 1-2 minutes at about 400°F in your preheated Air Fryer. Inspect the garlic, open the foil's top end, and keep cooking for an additional 10-12 minutes.

3. Once done, let them cool for around 10 to 15 minutes; take out the cloves by pressing them out of their skin; mash your garlic and put them aside.

4. Mix the salt, almond meal, and black pepper in a small dish.

5. Beat the eggs until foamy in a separate bowl.

6. Put some parmesan cheese in the final shallow dish.

7. In your almond meal blend, dip the avocado wedges, dusting off any excess.

8. In the beaten egg, dunk your wedges; eventually, dip in some parmesan cheese.

9. Spray your avocado wedges on both sides with some cooking oil spray.

10. Cook for around 8 minutes in the preheated Air Fryer at about 395° F, flipping them over midway thru the cooking process.

11. In the meantime, mix the ingredients of your sauce with your cooked crushed garlic.

12. Split the avocado wedges between plates and cover with the sauce before serving. Enjoy!

14. Crispy Wings with Lemony Old Bay Spice

Preparation time: 10 minutes

Cooking time: 25 minutes

Servings: 4 people

Ingredients:

- Salt and pepper according to taste

- 3 pounds of vegan chicken wings

- 1 tsp. of lemon juice, freshly squeezed

- 1 tbsp. of old bay spices

- ¾ cup of almond flour

- ½ cup of butter

Directions:

1. For about 5 minutes, preheat your air fryer. Mix all your ingredients in a mixing dish, excluding the butter. Put in the bowl of an air fryer.

2. Preheat the oven to about 350°F and bake for around 25 minutes. Rock the fryer container midway thru the cooking process, also for cooking.

3. Drizzle with some melted butter when it's done frying. Enjoy!

15. Cold Salad with Veggies and Pasta

Preparation time: 30 minutes

Cooking time: 1 hour 35 minutes

Servings: 12 people

Ingredients:

- ½ cup of fat-free Italian dressing

- 2 tablespoons of olive oil, divided

- ½ cup of Parmesan cheese, grated

- 8 cups of cooked pasta

- 4 medium tomatoes, cut in eighths

- 3 small eggplants, sliced into ½-inch thick rounds

- 3 medium zucchinis, sliced into ½-inch thick rounds

- Salt, according to your taste.

Directions:

1. Preheat your Air fryer to about 355° F and oil the inside of your air fryer basket. In a dish, mix 1 tablespoon of olive oil and zucchini and swirl to cover properly.

2. Cook for around 25 minutes your zucchini pieces in your Air fryer basket. In another dish, mix your eggplants with a tablespoon of olive oil and toss to coat properly.

3. Cook for around 40 minutes your eggplant slices in your Air fryer basket. Re-set the Air Fryer temperature to about 320° F and put the tomatoes next in the ready basket.

4. Cook and mix all your air-fried vegetables for around 30 minutes. To serve, mix in the rest of the ingredients and chill for at least 2 hours, covered.

16. Zucchini and Minty Eggplant Bites

Preparation time: 15 minutes

Cooking time: 35 minutes

Servings: 8 people

Ingredients:

- 3 tbsp. of olive oil

- 1 pound of zucchini, peeled and cubed

- 1 pound of eggplant, peeled and cubed

- 2 tbsp. of melted butter

- 1 ½ tsp. of red pepper chili flakes

- 2 tsp. of fresh mint leaves, minced

Directions:

1. In a large mixing container, add all of the ingredients mentioned above.

2. Roast the zucchini bites and eggplant in your Air Fryer for around 30 minutes at about 300° F, flipping once or twice during the cooking cycle. Serve with some dipping sauce that's homemade.

17. Stuffed Potatoes

Preparation time: 15 minutes

Cooking time: 31 minutes

Servings: 4 people

Ingredients:

- 3 tbsp. of canola oil

- ½ cup of Parmesan cheese, grated

- 2 tbsp. of chives, chopped

- ½ of brown onion, chopped

- 1 tbsp. of butter

- 4 potatoes, peeled

Directions:

1. Preheat the Air fryer to about 390° F and oil the air fryer basket. Coat the canola oil on the potatoes and place them in your Air Fryer Basket.

2. Cook for around 20 minutes before serving on a platter. Halve each potato and scrape out the middle from each half of it.

3. In a frying pan, melt some butter over medium heat and add the onions. Sauté in a bowl for around 5 minutes and dish out.

4. Combine the onions with the middle of the potato, chives and half of the cheese. Stir well and uniformly cram the onion potato mixture into the potato halves.

5. Top and layer the potato halves in your Air Fryer basket with the leftover cheese. Cook for around 6 minutes before serving hot.

18. Paneer Cutlet

Preparation time: 5 minutes

Cooking time: 15 minutes

Servings: 1 people

Ingredients:

- ½ teaspoon of salt

- ½ teaspoon of oregano

- 1 small onion, finely chopped

- ½ teaspoon of garlic powder

- 1 teaspoon of butter

- ½ teaspoon of chai masala

- 1 cup of grated cheese

Directions:

1. Preheat the air fryer to about 350° F and lightly oil a baking dish. In a mixing bowl, add all ingredients and stir well. Split the mixture into cutlets and put them in an oiled baking dish.

2. Put the baking dish in your air fryer and cook your cutlets until crispy, around a minute or so.

19. Spicy Roasted Cashew Nuts

Preparation time: 10 Minutes

Cooking time: 20 Minutes

Servings: 4

Ingredients:

- 1/2 tsp. of ancho chili powder

- 1/2 tsp. of smoked paprika

- Salt and ground black pepper, according to taste

- 1 tsp. of olive oil

- 1 cup of whole cashews

Directions:

1. In a mixing big bowl, toss all your ingredients.

2. Line parchment paper to cover the Air Fryer container. Space out the spiced cashews in your basket in a uniform layer.

3. Roast for about 6 to 8 minutes at 300 degrees F, tossing the basket once or twice during the cooking process. Work in batches if needed. Enjoy!

CHAPTER 4: Deserts

1. Almond-apple Treat

Preparation time: 5 minutes

Cooking time: 15 minutes

Servings: 4 people

Ingredients:

- 2 tablespoon of sugar

- ¾ oz. of raisins

- 1 ½ oz. of almonds

Directions:

1. Preheat your air fryer to around 360° F.

2. Mix the almonds, sugar, and raisins in a dish. Blend using a hand mixer.

3. Load the apples with a combination of the almond mixture. Please put them in the air fryer basket and cook for a few minutes. Enjoy!

2. Pepper-pineapple With Butter-sugar Glaze

Preparation time: 5 minutes

Cooking time: 10 minutes

Servings: 2 people

Ingredients:

- Salt according to taste.

- 2 tsp. of melted butter

- 1 tsp. of brown sugar

- 1 red bell pepper, seeded and julienned

- 1 medium-sized pineapple, peeled and sliced

Directions:

1. To about 390°F, preheat your air fryer. In your air fryer, put the grill pan attachment.

2. In a Ziploc bag, combine all ingredients and shake well.

3. Dump and cook on the grill pan for around 10 minutes to ensure you turn the pineapples over every 5 minutes during cooking.

3. True Churros with Yummy Hot Chocolate

Preparation time: 10 minutes

Cooking time: 25 minutes

Servings: 3 people

Ingredients:

- 1 tsp. of ground cinnamon

- 1/3 cup of sugar

- 1 tbsp. of cornstarch

- 1 cup of milk

- 2 ounces of dark chocolate

- 1 cup of all-purpose flour

- 1 tbsp. of canola oil

- 1 tsp. of lemon zest

- 1/4 tsp. of sea salt

- 2 tbsp. of granulated sugar

- 1/2 cup of water

Directions:

1. To create the churro dough, boil the water in a pan over a medium-high flame; then, add the salt, sugar, and lemon zest and fry, stirring continuously, until fully dissolved.

2. Take the pan off the heat and add in some canola oil. Stir the flour in steadily, constantly stirring until the solution turns to a ball.

3. With a broad star tip, pipe the paste into a piping bag. In the oiled Air Fryer basket, squeeze 4-inch slices of dough. Cook for around 6 minutes at a temperature of 300° F.

4. Make the hot cocoa for dipping in the meantime. In a shallow saucepan, melt some chocolate and 1/2 cup of milk over low flame.

5. In the leftover 1/2 cup of milk, mix the cornstarch and blend it into the hot chocolate mixture. Cook for around 5 minutes on low flame.

6. Mix the sugar and cinnamon; roll your churros in this combination. Serve with a side of hot cocoa. Enjoy!

Conclusion

These times, air frying is one of the most common cooking techniques and air fryers have become one of the chef's most impressive devices. In no time, air fryers can help you prepare nutritious and tasty meals! To prepare unique dishes for you and your family members, you do not need to be a master in the kitchen.

Everything you have to do is buy an air fryer and this wonderful cookbook for air fryers! Soon, you can make the greatest dishes ever and inspire those around you.

Cooked meals at home with you! Believe us! Get your hands on an air fryer and this handy set of recipes for air fryers and begin your new cooking experience. Have fun!

The Healthy Air Fryer Cookbook with Pictures

70+ Fried Tasty Recipes to Kill Hunger, Be Super Energetic and Make Your Day Brighter

By Giovanni Paletto

Table of Contents:

Introduction

An air fryer is a little kitchen appliance which imitates the outcomes of deep frying foods with the excess grease. As opposed to submerging food in order to fry it, the more food is put within the fryer together with a rather tiny quantity of oil. The food is subsequently "fried" having just hot air cooking. Food is cooked fast Because of the high heat and, because of the small quantity of oil onto the exterior of the meals, the outside will be emptied, like it was fried!

So, here we have discussed 70 best and healthy recipes for you that you can try at home and enjoy cooking using an air fryer.

Chapter 1: Air fryer Basics and 20 Recipes

Type of air fryer:

There're some air fryers that are over $300 and the one I used was less than a hundred. I didn't want you to splurge on the expensive one immediately because I was like what if I don't even use this thing? I want you to know that I'm going to use it first so I bought this for less than $100. This one is perfectly fine. It's big, it cooks a lot and it works just as good if not better than the more expensive models.

I'm going to bring you many air fryer recipes that are super easy. Even though it takes up quite a bit of counter space, it does a good job getting things crispy and delicious. Let's start with four recipes i.e. Bacon, Brussels sprouts, chicken wings and chicken breasts. So, let's get started.

1. Air fryer Bacon Recipe

I'm going to use four slices of bacon and I'm going to cut them in half on the cutting board.

So, here's the air fryer that I have:

It is a 5.7 quart which is a pretty large air fryer. You take out the drawer and then we're going to lay the bacon inside of the air fryer, as it all fits. You want it to be a single layer so that they get evenly cooked. We're going to put this back in so we set the temperature for 350 degrees and they will cook for about nine minutes. We will also check them a couple of times just to make sure they're not getting too overdone. That's all there is to it, so our air fryer bacon is already and let's pull it out.

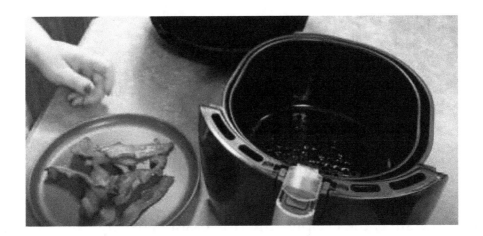

If you wanted it a little crispy, you could leave it in for probably just one more minute but I like it like this.

2. Air Fryer Apple Pie Chips

Let us be honest: If you are craving super-crispy, crunchy apple chips, then baking them in the oven is not good for you. The air fryer, on the other hand, is best.

You'll begin by slicing an apple (any variety will probably work, although a red apple generates extra-pretty processors), and in case you've got a mandolin, utilize it as the thinner the slice, the crispier the processor. Toss the pieces with cinnamon and nutmeg, put an even coating into a preheated air fryer, coat with cooking spray, and stir fry until golden. You will have a tasty snack in under 10 minutes. For maximum crunchiness, let cool completely before eating.

Ingredients

- Moderate red apple

- 1/4 tsp ground nutmeg

- 1/2 tsp ground cinnamon

- Cooking spray

Instructions

- ❏ Thinly slice the apple into 1/8-inch-thick slices using a knife or rather on a mandoline.

❏ Toss the apple slices with 1/2 teaspoon ground cinnamon along with 1/4 teaspoon ground nutmeg.

❏ Preheat in an air fryer into 375ºF and place for 17 minutes. Coat the fryer basket with cooking spray. Put just one layer of apple pieces into a basket and then spray with cooking spray.

❏ Air fry until golden-brown, rotating the trays halfway through to keep the apples at level, about 7 minutes total.

❏ Allow the chips to cool entirely too crisp.

❏ Repeat with the air fryer for the remaining apple pieces.

3. **Air-fryer Chicken Wings**

We will get started on the chicken wings.

Ingredients:

- 12 Chicken wings

- Salt

- Pepper

Method:

I'm going to put them in the air fryer basket and then I'm going to season them with salt and pepper. I've got these all in a single layer and they're kind of snug in there which is fine because they're going to shrink as they cook.

I put in about 12 chicken wings fit in my air fryer basket and now we're going to cook them for 25 minutes at 380 degrees. What that's going to do is it really get them cooked and then we're going to bump up the temperature and we will get them crispy. The first cook on our wings is done and now we are going to put it back in the air fryer at 400 degrees for about three to five minutes to get them nice and crispy. With this recipe and most air fryer recipes, whenever you're cooking things for longer than I would say five minutes, you may want to pull the basket out and shake what's inside. It is to make sure that it gets evenly cooked and I like to do that about every five minutes. Our wings are done. Look at how good they look in there nice and crispy.

This took about three minutes as I didn't have to do the full five minutes for these.

4. **Air Fryer Mini Breakfast Burritos**

All these air-fried miniature burritos are fantastic to get a catch's go breakfast or perhaps to get a midday snack. Leave the serrano Chile pepper for a spicy version.

Ingredients

- 1 tablespoon bacon grease

- 1/4 cup Mexican-style chorizo

- 2 tbsp. sliced onion

- 1 serrano pepper, chopped

- salt and ground black pepper to taste

- 4 (8 inch) flour tortillas

- 1/2 cup diced potatoes

- 2 large eggs

- avocado oil cooking spray

Instructions

- ❖ Cook chorizo in an air fryer over medium-high heat, stirring often, until sausage operates into a dark crimson, 6 to 8 minutes.

- ❖ Melt bacon grease in precisely the exact way over medium-high warmth.

- ❖ Add onion and serrano pepper and continue stirring and cooking until berries are fork-tender, onion is translucent, and serrano pepper is tender in 2 to 6 minutes.

- ❖ Add eggs and chorizo; stir fry till cooked and fully integrated into curry mixture in about 5 minutes. Season with pepper and salt.

- ❖ Meanwhile, heat tortillas directly onto the grates of a gasoline stove until pliable and soft.

- ❖ Put 1/3 cup chorizo mixture down the middle of each tortilla.

❖ Fold top and bottom of tortillas over the filling, then roll into a burrito form. Mist with cooking spray and put in the basket of a fryer.

❖ Flip each burrito above, peppermint with cooking spray, and fry until lightly browned, 2 to 4 minutes longer.

5. Herb Chicken Breast

Now let's get to the herb chicken breast.

Ingredients

- Salt

- Pepper

- Chicken Breast

- Smoked Paprika

- Butter

Method:

We've got two chicken breasts. We've got butter, Italian seasoning salt, pepper and smoked paprika. We're going to mix all of that into the butter to give it a quick mix. Now we've got our two chicken breasts here and we're going to spread the mixture over each chicken breast to give it a nice flavorful crust.

Put these in the air fryer with some tongs. We're ready to cook these in the air fryer.

Cook them at 370 degrees for about 10 to 15 minutes and then check it with a meat thermometer to make sure that they're perfectly cooked. Because we don't want them to be overcooked, then they'll be dry and we definitely don't want them to be undercooked.

Okay, we pulled our chicken out of the air fryer. We had one chicken breast that was smaller so it came out a little bit earlier and now we have this one that's ready and its right at 165. So, we know that our chickens are not going to be dry. Let's cut into one of these. Those are perfectly cooked and juicy

6. Three Cheese Omelet

Ingredients

- 3 Tbsp. heavy whipping cream

- ½ tsp salt

- 4 eggs

- ¼ cup cheddar cheese, grated

- ¼ cup provolone cheese

- ¼ tsp ground black pepper

- ¼ cup feta cheese

Method:

❖ Preheat your air fryer to 350 degrees F and line a baking pan using parchment paper. Be sure the pan will fit on your fryer- normally a seven inch round pan will do the job flawlessly.

❖ In a small bowl, whisk together the eggs, cream, pepper and salt

❖ Pour the mixture into the prepared baking pan then place the pan on your preheated air fryer.

❖ Cook for approximately ten minutes or till the eggs are completely set.

❖ Sprinkle the cheeses round the boiled eggs and then return the pan into the air fryer for one more moment to melt the cheese.

7. Patty Pan Frittata

I had a gorgeous patty pan squash sitting on my counter tops and was wondering exactly what to do with this was fresh and yummy for my loved ones. I had not made breakfast however so a summer squash frittata appeared in order! Comparable to zucchini, patty pan squash leant itself well to my fundamental frittata recipe. Serve with your favorite brunch sides or independently. You could also cool and serve cold within 24 hours.

Ingredients

- 1 patty pan squash

- 1 tbsp. unsalted butter

- 4 large eggs

- 1/4 cup crumbled goat cheese

- 1/4 cup grated Parmesan cheese

- salt and ground black pepper to taste

- 1/4 cup

- 2 medium scallions, chopped, green and white parts split

- 1 tsp garlic, minced

- 1 small tomato, seeded and diced

- 1 tsp hot sauce, or to flavor

Instructions

- ❖ Press 5-inch squares of parchment paper to 8 cups of a muffin tin, creasing where essential.

- ❖ Heat butter over moderate heat; stir fry into patty pan, scallion whites, salt, garlic, and pepper. Transfer into a bowl and set aside.

- ❖ Add sausage in the identical way and cook until heated through, about 3 minutes. Add sausage into patty pan mix.

- ❖ Fold in goat milk, Parmesan cheese, and tomato. Add hot sauce and season with pepper and salt. Twist in patty pan-sausage mix. Put frittata mixture to the prepared muffin cups, filling to the peak of every cup and then overfilling only when the parchment paper may encourage the mix.

❖ Put muffin tin in addition to a cookie sheet in the middle of the toaster.

8. Bacon and Cheese Frittata

Ingredients

- ½ cup cheddar cheese, grated

- 4 eggs

- ½ cup chopped, cooked bacon

- ½ tsp salt

- 3 Tbsp. heavy whipping cream

- ¼ tsp ground black pepper

Method:

- ❖ Preheat your air fryer to 350 degrees F and line a baking pan using parchment paper. Be sure the pan will fit on your fryer- normally a seven inch round pan will do the job flawlessly.

- ❖ In a small bowl, whisk together the eggs, cream, pepper and salt

- ❖ Stir in the cheese and bacon into the bowl.

- ❖ Pour the mixture into the prepared baking pan then place the pan on your preheated air fryer.

- ❖ Cook for approximately 15 minutes or till the eggs are completely set.

9. Meat Lovers Omelet

Ingredients:

- ¼ cup cheddar cheese, grated

- ¼ cup cooked, crumbled bacon

- ½ tsp salt

- 4 eggs

- ¼ cup cooked, crumbled sausage

- 3 Tbsp. heavy whipping cream

- ¼ tsp ground black pepper

Method:

- ❑ Preheat your air fryer to 350 degrees F and line a baking pan using parchment paper. Be sure the pan will fit on your fryer- normally a seven inch round pan will do the job flawlessly.

❑ In a small bowl whisk together the eggs, cream, pepper and salt.

❑ Pour the mixture into the prepared baking pan then place the pan on your preheated air fryer.

❑ Cook for approximately ten minutes or till the eggs are completely set.

❑ Sprinkle the cheeses round the boiled eggs and then return the pan into the fryer for another two minutes to melt the cheese.

10. Crispy Brussels sprouts

Next on our list is air fryer crispy Brussels sprouts.

Ingredients:

- Brussels sprouts

- Salt

- Pepper

Method:

Let's get started with these Brussels sprouts. Use fresh Brussels sprouts and we could also use frozen ones. I've got a bag of frozen Brussels sprouts and actually they're still broke. I'm going to season them with some salt and some pepper.

Shake them up and now I'm going to cook them at 400 or I'm going to start with 10 minutes. Let's see how it goes. I think you're going to be surprised because they're crispy. Can you believe that? I think these are better than fresh ones.

Use frozen if you want to make air fryer Brussels sprouts because the fresh ones take forever to get soft on the inside. You got to cut them into quarters, you've got to trim the leaves off these. They're frozen. I just threw them in the air fryer for 15minutes and they're good to go.

Now what I'm going to show you are actually dessert ideas that you can cook in your air fryer. They come in different sizes and one and a half liter is quite common too, so just check when you buy your own if you do that.

It is a bigger liter air fryer because I promise you, you're going to want to cook everything in this. What I love about this style of air fryer is that it's so simple on the front. You will see that you have got different settings but if you want to cook chips, prawns, fish, steak and muffins as well, it's really easy to adjust the temperature up and down. Also the time up and down as well. Then once you put your tray back in, all you need to do is select your setting and press the play button and the air fryer does everything else for you. It is also really really easy to clean. All you need to do is remove your tray from your air fryer, press the button on at the handle and detach your basket from the tray.

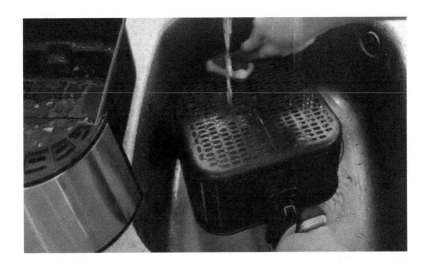

I then use a handheld scrubbing brush which dispenses washing-up liquid and I just go over my basket and my outer tray as well which is where all the fats from your food drip. I just go in with some warm water and my washing up liquid washes it all away. It's got a really nice TEFL coating so everything just wipes off. It's nonstick, then I just leave it on the side, let it dry and then pop it back in my air fryer. At once it is dry, so with all that said I'm just going to jump straight on into the recipes.

11.Hard Boiled Eggs

Ingredients:

- 4 eggs

Method:

➢ Preheat your air fryer to 250 degrees F.

➢ Place a wire rack in the fryer and set the eggs in addition to the rack.

➢ Cook for 17 minutes then remove the eggs and put them into an

➢ Ice water bath to cool and then stop the cooking procedure.

➢ Peel the eggs and love!

1. Spinach Parmesan Baked Eggs

Ingredients:

- 1 Tbsp. frozen, chopped spinach, thawed

- 1 Tbsp. grated parmesan cheese

- 2 eggs

- 1 Tbsp. heavy cream

- ¼ tsp salt

- 1/8 tsp ground black pepper

Method:

❏ Preheat your air fryer to 330 degrees F.

❏ Spray a silicone muffin cup or a little ramekin with cooking spray.

❏ In a small bowl, whisk together all of the components

❏ Pour the eggs into the ready ramekin and bake for 2 minutes.

❏ Enjoy directly from the skillet!

12. Fried hushpuppies.

Inside my home, stuffing is consistently the very popular Thanksgiving dish on the table. Because of this, we create double the amount we all actually need just so we can eat leftovers for a week! And while remaining stuffing alone is yummy, turning it into hushpuppies? Now that is only pure wizardry. Here is the way to use your air fryer to produce near-instant two-ingredient fried hushpuppies.

Ingredients:

- large egg

- cold stuffing

- Cooking spray

Directions:

★ Put 1 large egg in a large bowl and gently beat. Add 3 cups leftover stuffing and stir till blended.

★ Preheat in an air fryer into 355ºF and place it for 12 minutes. Put one layer of hushpuppies on the racks and then spray the tops with cooking spray.

★ Repeat with the remaining mixture.

13.**Keto Breakfast Pizza**

An egg, sausage, and pork rind "crust" holds sauce, cheese, and other savory toppings within this keto-friendly breakfast pizza recipe.

Ingredients

- 3 large eggs, split

- 2 tbsp. Italian seasoning

- 1 cup ready country-style sauce

- 10 tbsp. bacon pieces

- 1 pound bulk breakfast sausage

- cooking spray

- 1/3 cup crushed pork rinds

- 2 tbsp. chopped yellow onion

- 2 tbsp. diced jalapeno pepper

- 1 cup shredded Cheddar cheese

Instructions

★ Grease a rimmed pizza sheet.

★ Spread mixture out on the pizza sheet at a big, thin circle.

★ Meanwhile, spray a large air fryer with cooking spray and heat over medium-high heat. Whisk remaining eggs together in a bowl and then pour into it.

★ Place an oven rack about 6 inches from the heat source and then turn on the oven's broiler.

★ Spread sausage evenly over the beef "crust", sprinkle scrambled eggs. Sprinkle with bacon pieces, onion, and jalapeno.

★ Broil pizza in the preheated oven till cheese is melted, bubbling, and lightly browned, 3 to 5 minutes. Let cool and cut into fourths prior to serving.

14. Mozzarella stick

Ready for the simplest mozzarella stick recipe? These air fryer mozzarella sticks are created completely from pantry and refrigerator staples (cheese sticks and breadcrumbs), which means that you can dig to the crispy-coated, nostalgic bite anytime you would like.

INGREDIENTS:

➤ 1 (12-ounce) bundle mayonnaise

➤ 1 large egg

➤ 1/2 tsp garlic powder

➤ all-purpose flour

➤ 1/2 tsp onion powder

Method:

★ Before frying pan, set the halved cheese sticks onto a rimmed baking sheet lined with parchment paper. Freeze for half an hour. Meanwhile, construct the breading and get outside the air fryer.

★ Whisk the egg and lettuce together in a skillet. Put the flour, breadcrumbs, onion, and garlic powder in a large bowl and whisk to mix.

★ Working in batches of 6, then roll the suspended cheese sticks at the mayo-egg mix to coat, and then in the flour mixture.

★ Pour the coated cheese sticks into the parchment-lined baking sheet. Pour the baking sheet into the freezer for 10 minutes.

★ Heat the fryer to 370°F. Fry 6 the mozzarella sticks for 5 minutes -- it's important not to overcrowd the fryer.

★ Repeat with the rest of the sticks and serve hot with the marinara for dipping.

15. Raspberry Muffins

Ingredients:

- ¼ cup whole milk

- 1 egg

- 1 Tbsp. powdered stevia

- ¼ tsp salt

- ¼ tsp ground cinnamon

- 1 ½ tsp baking powder

- 1 cup almond flour

- ½ cup frozen or fresh raspberries

Steps:

I. Preheat your air fryer to 350 degrees F.

II. In a large bowl, stir together the almond milk, stevia, salt, cinnamon, and baking powder.

III. Add the milk and eggs and then stir well.

IV. Split the muffin batter involving each muffin cup, filling roughly 3/4 of this way complete.

V. Set the muffins to the fryer basket and cook for 14 minutes or till a toothpick comes out when inserted to the middle.

VI.   Eliminate from the fryer and let cool.

16. Sausage Tray Bake

I have just chopped up some new potatoes and then I've got some chipolata sausages so I'm going to make a tray bake.

Ingredients:

- Potatoes

- Chipolata Sausage

- corvette

- Onion

- Garlic

Method:

I would put potato and chipotle sausage into the air fryer for about 20 minutes at first before I add in my other veggies.

Once these have been in for 20 minutes or so, I will then add in two papers of corvette, an onion and some garlic to go in as well. Cook them for a further 10 minutes and then dinner should be ready.

17. Strawberry Muffins

Ingredients:

- ¼ cup whole milk

- 1 ½ tsp baking powder

- ½ cup chopped strawberries

- 1 egg

- ¼ tsp salt

- ¼ tsp ground cinnamon

- 1 cup almond flour

- 1 Tbsp. powdered stevia

Steps:

1. Preheat your air fryer to 350 degrees F.

2. In a large bowl, stir together the almond milk, stevia, salt, cinnamon, and baking powder.

3. Add the milk and eggs and then stir well.

4. Fold in the berries.

5. Split the muffin batter involving each muffin cup, filling roughly 3/4 of this way complete.

6. Set the muffins to the fryer basket and cook for 14 minutes or till a toothpick comes out when inserted to the middle.

7. Eliminate from the fryer and let cool.

18. Bacon and Eggs for a single

Ingredients:

- 1 Tbsp. heavy cream

- two Tbsp. cooked, crumbled bacon

- 1/4 tsp salt

- 2 eggs

- 1/8 tsp ground black pepper

Directions

❏ Preheat your air fryer to 330 degrees F.

❏ Spray a silicone muffin cup or a little ramekin with cooking spray.

❏ In a small bowl, whisk together all of the components

❏ Pour the eggs into the ready ramekin and bake for 2 minutes.

❏ Enjoy directly from the skillet!

19. Mini Sausage Pancake Skewers with Spicy Syrup

These small savory skewers are fantastic for breakfast or a fantastic addition to your brunch buffet. The hot maple syrup garnish kicks up the flavor and adds some zest to sandwiches and sausage.

Ingredients

Syrup:

- 4 tbsp. unsalted butter

- 1/2 tsp salt

- 1/2 cup maple syrup

- 1 tsp red pepper flakes, or to taste

Pancake

- 1 cup buttermilk

- 2 tbsp. unsalted butter, melted

- 1 cup all-purpose flour

- 1 large egg

- 1 tbsp. olive oil

- 1 lb. ounce standard pork sausage (like Jimmy Dean®)

- 13 4-inch bamboo skewers

- 2 tablespoons sour cream

- 1/2 tbsp. brown sugar

- 1/4 tsp baking powder

- 1/4 tsp salt

- 2 tsp maple syrup

Instructions

- ❏ Bring to a boil and cook for 3 to 4 minutes.

❏ Meanwhile, prepare pancakes: whisk flour, sugar, baking powder, and salt in a huge bowl. Whisk buttermilk, egg, sour cream, melted butter and maple syrup together in another bowl. Pour the wet ingredients into the flour mixture. Stir lightly until just blended but slightly lumpy; don't overmix. Let sit for 10 minutes.

❏ Heat in an air fryer over moderate heat. Drop teaspoonfuls of batter onto them to make 1-inch diameter sandwiches.

❏ Cook for approximately 1 to 2 minutes, then reverse, and keep cooking until golden brown, about 1 minute. Transfer cooked pancakes into a plate and repeat with remaining batter.

❏ Heat olive oil at precisely the exact same fryer over moderate heat. Form table-spoonfuls of sausage to 1-inch patties, exactly the exact same size as the miniature pancakes.

❏ Cook until patties are cooked through, about 3 minutes each side. Transfer to a newspaper towel-lined plate.

❏ Blend 3 pancakes and two sausage patties onto each skewer, beginning and end with a pancake.

❏ Repeat to create staying skewers. Serve drizzled with hot syrup.

20. Avocado Baked Eggs

Ingredients:

- 1 Tbsp. heavy cream

- ¼ tsp salt

- ¼ avocado, diced

- 1 Tbsp. grated cheddar cheese

- 2 eggs

- 1/8 tsp ground black pepper

Method:

❏ Preheat your air fryer to 330 degrees F.

❏ Spray a silicone muffin cup or a little ramekin with cooking spray.

❏ In a small bowl, whisk together the eggs, cream, cheddar cheese, salt, and pepper.

❏ Stir in the avocado and pour the eggs into the ready ramekin and bake for 2 minutes.

❏ Enjoy directly from the skillet!

Chapter 2: Air Fryer 50 more Recipes for You!

21. Sausage and Cheese Omelet

Ingredients:

- ¼ cup cheddar cheese, grated

- ½ cup cooked, crumbled sausage

- 4 eggs

- 3 Tbsp. heavy whipping cream

- ½ tsp salt

- ¼ tsp ground black pepper

Method

01. Preheat your air fryer to 320 degrees F and line a baking pan using parchment paper. Be sure the pan will fit on your fryer- normally a seven inch round pan will do the job flawlessly.

02. In a small bowl, whisk together the eggs, cream, pepper and salt.

03. Pour the mixture into the prepared baking pan then place the pan on your preheated air fryer.

04. Cook for approximately ten minutes or till the eggs are completely set.

05. Sprinkle the cheeses round the boiled eggs and then return the pan into the fryer for another two minutes to melt the cheese.

22. Pita bread Pizza

I am making some pita bread pizzas now.

Ingredients:

- Bread

- Tomato puree

- Passat

Method:

I usually would make these in the oven and I would put them in there for about 10 to 15 minutes. I'm just going to put some ketchup on top of the pizza bread base.

Or you can put tomato puree on there or some pasta whatever you've got. Then I'm just going to put some cheese on really nice and simple. I'm going to pop them on the pizza setting in the air fryer so that's eight minutes when I do my pizzas in the oven the base isn't really nice and crispy. So, I am really pleased with how they've turned out in the air fryer. Pizzas are done, crispy delicious, ready to eat.

23. Air Fryer Hanukkah Latkes

If you have never needed a latke, it is about time we change this. Traditionally served throughout Hanukkah, these crispy fritters -- frequently made with grated potatoes, lettuce, onion, and matzo meal -- are kind of impossible to not love.

Traditionally latkes are fried in oil (or poultry schmaltz!)) , however I wanted to see if I could create them using the popular air fryer. Since the fryer is a high-heat convection oven, the large fan speed and focused warmth yields a crispy potato pancake that is also soft at the middle.

INGREDIENTS

- 1 1/2 Pounds Russet potatoes (2 to 3 tbsp.)

- ½ medium yellow onion

- 1/2 tsp freshly ground black pepper

- Cooking spray

- Two large eggs

- matzo meal

- 2 tsp kosher salt

Description:

❖ Peel 1 1/2 lbs. russet potatoes. Grate the potatoes and 1/2 yellow onion onto the large holes of a box grater. Put with a clean kitchen towel, then pull up the sides of the towel to make a package, and squeeze out excess moisture.

❖ Transfer the curry mixture into a large bowl. Add two large eggs, 1/4 cup matzo meal, two tsp kosher salt, and 1/2 tsp black pepper, and stir to blend.

❖ Preheat the Air Fryer into 375°F and place it for 16 minutes. Coat the air fryer racks together with cooking spray.

❖ Dip the latke mix in 2-tablespoon dollops to the fryer, flattening the shirts to make a patty.

❖ Air fry, rotating the trays halfway through, for 2 minutes total. Repeat with the rest of the latke mix.

24. Salmon Fillet

Now, I'm going to cook some salmon in it.

Ingredients:

- Salmon

Method:

I put my salmon in, with nothing on top of it, just a salmon filet. I pop it in on the fish sitting for ten minutes and when it comes out it has got the crispy skin ever. The salmon was in for ten minutes and I wanted to show you how crispy the skin is.

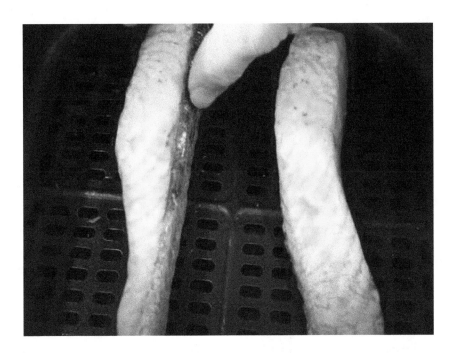

I'm someone who loves eating salmon skin and that is just perfectly done right.

25. Air Fryer Mini Calzones

Among the greatest approaches to utilize an air fryer is a miniature oven that will not heat up your entire kitchen for party snacks. It's possible to turn out batch after batch of wings, mozzarella sticks, and also, yes, miniature calzones which are hot, crispy, and superbly nostalgic by one air fryer.

These mini calzones utilize ready pizza dough to produce delicious pockets full of gooey cheese, piquant tomato sauce, and hot pepperoni that are fantastic for celebrations, after-school snacks, or even for satisfying your craving to get your dessert rolls of your childhood.

Ingredients:

- All-purpose flour, for rolling the dough out

- Pizza sauce, and more for dipping

- Thinly sliced pepperoni

- miniature pepperoni, chopped

Directions:

- ❖ Utilize a 3-inch round cutter or a large glass to cut 8 to 10 rounds of bread.

- ❖ Transfer the rounds into some parchment paper-lined baking sheet. Gather up the dough scraps, then reroll and replicate cutting rounds out until you've got 16.

- ❖ Top each round with two tsp of sauce, 1 tablespoon of cheese, and one tsp of pepperoni.

- ❖ Working with a single dough around at a time, fold in half an hour, then pinch the edges together to seal. When every calzone is sealed, then use a fork to crimp the borders shut to additional seal.

❖ Heat the air fryer into 375°F. Working in batches of 4, air fry the calzones until golden brown and crispy, about 8 minutes. Serve with extra pizza sauce for dipping, if desired.

26. Fajitas

Ingredients:

- Turkey Strips

- Yellow Pepper

- Onion

- Orange Pepper

Method:

It's a night that we are going to be having for heaters. So, here, I've chopped up yellow and orange pepper and also half an onion. I have got some turkey strips.

I'll pass it over heat as it makes barbecue flavor onto all of this. So, I'm just going to pop these all into the air fryer together because I think they'll actually cook through at a very similar rate. Then I am going to pop them on the chicken setting and let the air fryer get cooking alright. This is the fajita mix in ten minutes.

I put on the chicken setting which is actually 20 minutes but I was just checking it.

I cut a piece of the turkey and it's perfect all the way through, I cut it like one of the biggest pieces up as well. So, it's absolutely perfect so all this needs is ten minutes in the air fryer and it's done right.

27. Pot Sweet Potato Chips

Replace the humble sweet potato to a freshly-fried bite, and it is sure to be yummy. Sweet potato chips, sweet potato tater tots -- you name it, we will take it.

The comparison between the sweetness of the curry and the saltiness of this bite is really impossible to not love.

These air fryer sweet potato chips provide everything you adore about these deep-fried snacks. That is the great thing about the air fryer that it requires less oil, after all -- you have to bypass the hassle and clutter of heating a massive pot of oil to the stove -- but the "fried" cure comes out evenly as yummy. And unlike a store-bought bag of chips, you have to personalize the seasonings. Here, we are using dried herbs and a pinch of cayenne for an earthy, somewhat spicy beverage.

Ingredients:

- medium sweet potato

- 1 tbsp. canola oil

- 1/2 tsp freshly ground black pepper

- 1/4 tsp paprika

- 1 tsp kosher salt

- 3/4 tsp dried thyme leaves

- Cooking spray

Directions:

❏ Wash 1 sweet potato and dry nicely. Thinly slice 1/8-inch thick using a knife or rather on a mandolin. Set in a bowl, then cover with cool water, and then soak at room temperature for 20 minutes to remove the excess starch.

❏ Drain the pieces and pat very dry with towels. Put into a large bowl, then add 1 tbsp. canola oil, 1 tsp kosher salt, 3/4 tsp dried thyme leaves, 1/2 tsp black pepper, 1/4 tsp paprika, and a pinch cayenne pepper if using, and toss to blend.

❑ Gently coat in an air fryer rotisserie basket with cooking spray.

❑ Air fry in batches: put one layer of sweet potato pieces from the rotisserie basket. Put the rotisserie basket at the fryer and press on.

❑ Preheat the fryer into 340ºF and place for 22 minutes, until the sweet potatoes are golden brown and the edges are crispy, 19 to 22 minutes.

❑ Transfer the chips into a newspaper towel-lined plate to cool completely

❑ They will crisp as they cool. Repeat with the remaining sweet potato pieces.

28. **Easy Baked Eggs**

Ingredients:

- 1 Tbsp. heavy cream

- ¼ tsp salt

- 2 eggs

- 1/8 tsp ground black pepper

Method:

➤ Preheat your fryer to 330 degrees F.

➤ Spray a silicone muffin cup or a little ramekin with cooking spray.

➤ In a small bowl, whisk together all of the components

➤ Pour the eggs into the ready ramekin and bake for 6 minutes.

➤ Enjoy directly from the skillet!

29. Air Fryer Buttermilk Fried Chicken

I went to school in the South, so I have had my fair share of crispy, succulent, finger-licking fried chicken. As you might imagine, I had been skeptical about creating a much healthier version from the air fryer.

The second I pulled out my first batch, but my worries disappeared. The epidermis was crispy, the coat was cracker-crisp (as it ought to be), and also, above all, the chicken itself was tender and succulent -- the indication of a perfect piece of fried chicken.

Air fryer fried chicken is lighter, quicker, than and not as cluttered as deep-fried chicken. Here is the way to get it done.

Ingredients

- 1 tsp Freshly ground black pepper, divided

- Buttermilk

- 1 tsp Cayenne pepper

- 1 tbsp. Garlic powder

- 2 tbsp. paprika

- 1 tbsp. onion powder

- 1 tsp kosher salt, divided

- all-purpose flour

- 1 tbsp. ground mustard

- Cooking spray

Directions

- ❏ Put all ingredients into a large bowl and season with 1 teaspoon of the kosher salt and 1/2 tsp of honey.

- ❏ Add 2 cups buttermilk and simmer for 1 hour in the fridge. Meanwhile, whisk the remaining 1 tbsp. kosher salt, staying 1/2 tsp black pepper, 2 cups all-purpose flour, 1 tbsp. garlic powder, 2 tbsp. paprika, 1 teaspoon cayenne pepper, 1 tbsp. onion powder, plus one tbsp. ground mustard together into a huge bowl.

❏ Preheat an air fryer into 390°F. Coat the fryer racks together with cooking spray. Remove the chicken in the buttermilk, allowing any excess to drip off. Dredge in the flour mixture, shaking off any excess. Put one layer of chicken in the basket, with distance between the bits. Air fry, turning the chicken hallway through, until an instant-read thermometer registers 165°F from the thickest part

❏ Cook for 18 to 20 minutes, then complete.

30. Keto Chocolate Chip Muffins

Ingredients:

- ¼ tsp salt

- 1 Tbsp. powdered stevia

- ¼ cup whole milk

- 1 egg

- 1 cup almond flour

- 1 ½ tsp baking powder

- ½ cup mini dark chocolate chips (sugar free)

Method:

❖ Preheat your air fryer to 350 degrees F.

❖ In a large bowl, stir together the almond milk, stevia, salt, cinnamon, and baking powder.

❖ Add the milk and eggs and then stir well.

❖ Split the muffin batter involving each muffin cup, filling around 3/4 of this way complete.

❖ Set the muffins to the air fryer basket and cook for 14 minutes or till a toothpick comes out when put to the middle.

❖ Eliminate from the fryer and let cool.

31. Crispy Chickpeas

What, I've got in here are some chickpeas.

Ingredients:

- Chickpeas

- Olive oil

- Per-peril salt

Method:

I've drained and washed chickpeas and then what I'm going to do is add on some olive oil and then also the periphery salt. The reason I put some olive oil on is because it just helps the pair of results stick to the chickpeas.

Then I'm just going to mix everything in together and pop them into the air fryer for about 15 minutes. On the chip setting these are great little snacks to make like pre dinner snacks. Instead of having crisps or if you're watching a movie, instead of having popcorn these are good little things. Also, if you are having a salad they're really nice to go in your salad as well.

32. Keto Blueberry Muffins

Ingredients:

- 1 egg

- ¼ tsp salt

- 1 cup almond flour

- 1 Tbsp. powdered stevia

- 1 ½ tsp baking powder

- ¼ cup whole milk

- ¼ tsp ground cinnamon

- ½ cup frozen or fresh blueberries

Steps:

1) Preheat your air fryer to 350 degrees F.

2) In a large bowl, stir together the almond milk, stevia, salt, cinnamon, and baking powder.

3) Add the milk and eggs and then stir well.

4) Split the muffin batter involving each muffin cup, filling roughly 3/4 of this way complete.

5) Set the muffins to the air fryer basket and cook for 14 minutes or till a toothpick comes out when put to the middle.

6) Eliminate from the fryer and let cool.

33. **Air Fryer Donuts**

Ingredients

- ground cinnamon

- granulated sugar

- Flaky large snacks,

- Jojoba oil spray or coconut oil spray

Instructions

★ Combine sugar and cinnamon in a shallow bowl; place aside.

★ Remove the cookies from the tin, separate them and set them onto the baking sheet.

★ Utilize a 1-inch round biscuit cutter (or similarly-sized jar cap) to cut holes from the middle of each biscuit.

★ Lightly coat an air fryer basket using coconut or olive oil spray (don't use nonstick cooking spray like Pam, which may damage the coating onto the basket)

★ Put 3 to 4 donuts in one layer in the air fryer (that they shouldn't be touching). Close to the air fryer and place to 350°F. Transfer donuts into the baking sheet.

★ Repeat with the rest of the biscuits. You can also cook the donut holes they will take approximately 3 minutes total

★ Brush both sides of this hot donut with melted butter, put in the cinnamon sugar, and then turn to coat both sides.

34. Sausage and Spinach Omelet

Ingredients:

½ cup baby spinach

4 eggs

¼ cup cheddar cheese, grated

½ cup cooked, crumbled sausage

3 Tbsp. heavy whipping cream

½ tsp salt

¼ tsp ground black pepper

Directions

I.   Preheat the air fryer at around 330 F.

II.   In a small bowl, whisk together the eggs, cream, pepper and salt.

III.   Fold in the cooked sausage and sausage.

IV.   Pour the mixture into the prepared baking pan then place the pan on your

V.   Cook for approximately ten minutes or till the eggs are completely set.

VI.   Sprinkle the cheeses round the boiled eggs and then return the pan into the fryer

VII.   Fryer for another two minutes to melt the cheese.

35. **Air Fryer Potato Wedges**

Perfectly crisp and seasoned potato wedges directly from your air fryer. It will not get any simpler than this!

Ingredients

➔ 2 medium Russet potatoes, cut into wedges

➔ 1/2 tsp sea salt

➔ 1 1/2 tsp olive oil

➔ 1/2 tsp chili powder

➔ ⅛ teaspoon ground black pepper

➔ 1/2 tsp paprika

➔ 1/2 tsp parsley flakes

Instructions

❖ Place potato wedges in a large bowl.

❖ Put 8 wedges at the jar of the air fryer and cook for 10 minutes.

❖ Flip wedges with tongs and cook for another five minutes.

36. Chocolate Chip Cookies in Air fryer

They are my day pick-me-up, my after-dinner treat, also, sometimes, a part of my breakfast. I keep either frozen cookies or baked biscuits in my freezer -- true my friends know and have come to appreciate when they come around for dinner or even a glass of wine.

The kind of chocolate chip cookie I enjoy all, depends upon my mood. Sometimes I need them super doughy, and sometimes challenging and crisp. If you're searching for one someplace in between -- gooey on the inside and crunchy on the outside -- I have discovered the foolproof way of you. It entails cooking them on your air fryer.

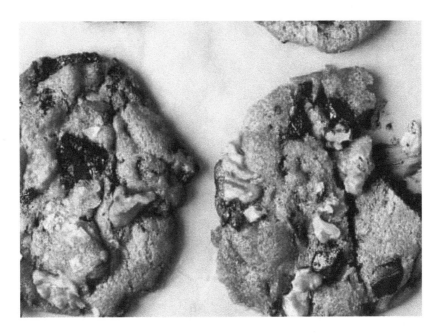

When using your fryer to create biscuits, be certain that you always line its base with foil to aid with simple cleanup. You will also need to line the basket or racks using parchment paper. Buy paper which has holes in it, cut some slits to the newspaper, or make sure you leave space around it which will allow for even cooking and flow of the air. With these suggestions, you're on your way to cookie victory!

Ingredients:

- Granulated sugar

- vanilla extract

- dark brown sugar

- 1 tsp kosher salt

- 2 large eggs

- 3/4 cup chopped walnuts

- 1 tsp baking soda

- Flaky sea salt, for garnish (optional)

- all-purpose flour

- Cooking spray

INSTRUCTIONS

❖ Put 2 sticks unsalted butter in the bowl of a stand mixer, fitted with the paddle attachment and also let it sit till softened. Insert 3/4 cup granulated sugar and 3/4 cup packed dark brown sugar and beat it on medium speed till blended and fluffy within 3 to 4 minutes. Add 1 tablespoon lemon extract, 2 big eggs, and 1 tsp kosher salt, and beat until just blended. After that, add 1 tea-spoon baking soda plus 2 1/3 cups all-purpose flour in increments, mixing until just blended.

❖ Add 2 cups chocolate balls and 3/4 cup chopped peppers and stir with a rubber spatula until just blended.

❖ Preheat in an air fryer, at 350ºF and set to 5 minutes. Line the fryer racks with parchment paper, make sure you leave space on all sides for air to leak.

❖ Reduce 2-tablespoon scoops of this dough on the racks, setting them 1-inch apart. Gently flatten each spade marginally to earn a cookie form.

❖ Sprinkle with flaky sea salt, if using. Bake until golden brown, about 5 minutes. Remove the racks out of the fryer and let it cool for 3 to 5 minutes to place. Repeat with the remaining dough.

37.Crispy Coated Veggies

Ingredients:

- Vegetables

- Egg

- Paprika

- Salt & Pepper

Method:

I'm making some crispy coating of vegetables in this bowl. I have got one egg beaten up. This is actually almond flour but you can use normal flour and then I popped in some paprika. I've also put in some salt and pepper here too. Then I'm going to dip my veggies into my egg and then I'll put them into the flour mixture, then into the air fryer for probably about eight minutes.

38. Ranch Pork Chops in Air fryer

Ingredients

- 4 boneless, center-cut pork chops, 1-inch thick

- aluminum foil

- cooking spray

- 2 Tsp dry ranch salad dressing mix

Directions

★ Put pork chops on a plate and then gently spray both sides with cooking spray. Sprinkle both sides with ranch seasoning mixture and let them sit at room temperature for 10 minutes.

★ Spray the basket of an air fryer with cooking spray and preheat at 390 degrees F (200 degrees C).

★ Place chops in the preheated air fryer, working in batches if needed, to guarantee the fryer isn't overcrowded.

★ Flip chops and cook for 5 minutes longer. Let rest on a foil-covered plate for 5 minutes prior to serving.

39.Quesadillas

Ingredients:

- Refried Beans

- Cheese

- Peppers

- Chicken

Method:

I'm going to be using the El Paso refried beans in the tin. I will spread that onto the wrap and then I'm just going to sprinkle some cheese on top.

This is a really basic wrap so usually when we have routes we'll add some like peppers in here as well and loads of other bits like chicken. I just wanted to show you how well they cook in the air fryer. You pop them in on the pizza setting and in 8 to10 minutes they are done. Really crispy and ready to eat.

40. Pecan Crusted Pork Chops at the Air Fryer

The air-fryer makes simple work of those yummy pork chops. The chops make good leftovers too, since the pecan crust does not get soggy!

Ingredients:

- Egg

- Pork

- Pecans

- Simmer

Instructions

➤ Add egg and simmer until all ingredients are well blended. Place pecans onto a plate.

➤ Dip each pork dip in the egg mix, then put onto the plate together with the pecans

➤ Press pecans firmly onto either side until coated. Spray the chops on both sides with cooking spray and set from the fryer basket.

➤ Cook at the fryer for 6 minutes. Turn chops closely with tongs, and fry until pork is no longer pink in the middle, about 6 minutes more.

41.Crispy Chicken Thighs

Ingredients

- Chicken thighs

- Pepper

- Olive oil

- Paprika

- Salt

Method:

I've got some chicken thighs. These have got bone-in and skinned on so what I've done is just put some olive oil on top of them with some paprika and some salt and pepper. Then I just rubbed everything into the chicken skin so I'm going to pop these into my air fryer. Press the chicken button and let the air fryer just do its thing.

This skin is super crispy that is perfectly done and it's been in there for 20 minutes. I just wanted to show you all the fat that came out of that chicken so here are all the oils that came off.

So those are what your chicken would be sitting in but instead it's all just tripped underneath the air fryer.

42. Bacon-Wrapped Scallops with Sirach Mayo

This yummy appetizer is ready quickly and easily in the air fryer and served with a hot Sirach mayo skillet. I use the smaller bay scallops because of this. If you're using jumbo scallops, it'll require a longer cooking time and more bits of bacon.

Ingredients

- 1/2 cup mayonnaise

- 1 pinch coarse salt

- 2 tbsp. Sirach sauce

- 1 pound bay scallops (about 36 small scallops)

- 1 pinch freshly cracked black pepper

- 12 slices bacon, cut into thirds

- 1 serving olive oil cooking spray

Instructions

★ Mix mayonnaise and Sirach sauce together in a little bowl.

★ Preheat the air fryer to 390 degrees F (200 degrees C).

★ Season with pepper and salt. Wrap each scallop with 1/3 piece of bacon and fasten with a toothpick.

★ Spray the air fryer basket with cooking spray. Put bacon-wrapped scallops from the basket in one layer; divide into two batches if needed.

★ Cook at the air fryer for 7 minutes. Check for doneness; scallops should be wheat and opaque ought to be crispy. Cook 1 to 2 minutes more, if needed, checking every moment. Remove scallops carefully with tongs and put on a newspaper towel-lined plate to absorb extra oil out of the bacon.

43.Homemade Chips

Ingredients

- Chip

- Olive oil

- Paprika

- Salt

Method:

Now I'm going to do some chips. I've just cut up some potatoes into chip shapes and then I am going to put some olive oil on top. Some paprika and some salt and the main reason I'm putting olive oil on top is basically for the paprika and the salt to stick to the surface of the chips. I'll just pop these in and then I'll put them onto the chip setting and let them cook away for about 18 minutes. I will be staring these halfway through because I'm doing quite a few chips as well. I will probably have to put these on for another 10 minutes after the 18 minutes is done.

44. Easy Air Fryer Pork Chops

Boneless pork chops cooked to perfection with the help of an air fryer. This recipe is super easy and you could not ask for a more tender and succulent chop.

Ingredients

- 1/2 cup grated Parmesan cheese

- 1 tsp kosher salt

- 4 (5 oz.) center-cut pork chops

- 2 tbsp. extra virgin olive oil

- 1 tsp dried parsley

- 1 tsp paprika

- 1 tsp garlic powder

- 1/2 teaspoon ground black pepper

Instructions

❏ Preheat the fryer to 390 degrees F.

❏ Combine Parmesan cheese, paprika, garlic powder, salt, parsley, and pepper in a level shallow dish; combine well.

❏ Stir every pork chop with olive oil. Dredge both sides of each dip from the Parmesan mixture and put on a plate.

❏ Put 2 chops from the basket of the fryer and cook for 10 minutes; turning halfway through cook time.

45. Corn on the Cob

Ingredients:

- Corn

- Butter

- Salt

Method:

We're going to do some corn on the cob. What I'm going to do is just pop them into my air fryer but not put anything on top of them. I'm going to put them in on the prawn settings.

It's just eight minutes, after ten minutes like I said, I will then add some butter on top and a little bit of salt. They're ready to eat.

46. Air Fryer Broiled Grapefruit

This hot and warm grapefruit with a buttery candy topping is the best accompaniment for your Sunday brunch and makes a lovely snack or dessert. I love to add a pinch of sea salt in the end to actually bring out the tastes.

Ingredients

- 1 red grapefruit, refrigerated

- aluminum foil

- 1 tbsp. brown sugar

- 1/2 teaspoon ground cinnamon

- 1 tbsp. softened butter

- 2 tsp sugar

Instructions

➢ Cut grapefruit in half crosswise and slice off a thin sliver away from the base of every half, when the fruit is not sitting at level. Use a sharp paring knife to cut around the outer edge of this grapefruit and involve every section to generate the fruit easier to consume after cooking.

➢ Combine softened butter 1 tbsp. brown sugar in a small bowl. Spread mix over each grapefruit in half. Sprinkle with remaining brown sugar levels.

➢ Cut aluminum foil into two 5-inch squares and put each grapefruit half one square; fold the edges up to catch any juices. Place in the air fryer basket.

➢ Broil in the fryer until the sugar mixture is bubbling, 6 to 7 minutes.

47.Kale Crisps

Ingredients:

- Kale

- Olive oil

- Salt

Method:

I'm going to make some kale crisps now. So, the first thing we're going to do list, get my kale and chop off the thick stocky bits. Once I've chopped that out, I will then just dice my kale up into kind of chunks and then I'll pop them into a bowl. Put some olive oil on top and some salts give everything a mix around.

I'll pop them into my air fryer and on the prong setting. The reason I put them on the prong setting is because that's just a quick eight minute setting and that's the perfect amount of time that these kale crisps take to cook. When they come out, they are super nice and crunchy and they taste delicious.

48. Air Fryer Brown Sugar and Pecan Roasted Apples

A sweet and nutty topping made with brown sugar and pecans adds amazing flavor to apples since they cook to tender perfection at the air fryer.

Ingredients

- 1/4 tsp apple pie spice

- 2 tbsp. coarsely chopped pecans

- 1 tbsp. brown sugar

- 1 tbsp. butter, melted

- 1 tsp all-purpose flour

- 2 medium apples, cored and cut into wedges

Instructions

➜ Preheat the air fryer to 350 degrees F

➜ Put apple wedges in a skillet drizzle with butter and toss to coat. Arrange apples in one layer in the air fryer basket and then sprinkle with pecan mixture.

➜ Cook in the preheated air fryer until apples are tender, 10 to 15 minutes.

49.Sausage Rolls

Ingredients:

- Sausage

- Puff pastry

- Cheese

- Chutney

- Milk

Methods:

Today we're going to make some really easy sausage rolls. So, I've just got some puff pastry and some sausages. What I'll do is I'll cut the puff pastry into four pieces. I'll then lay a sausage into each one of the pieces along with some grated cheese.

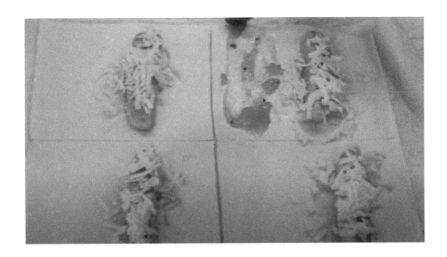

I like to have some chutney in the house as well. I'll just fold over the pastry and then secure it with a fork at the edges. So, it doesn't open up. I then just also get a bit of milk as well or you can use a beaten egg and just brush it over the top so it goes nice and golden brown. I'll pop it into my air fryer on the chip setting because they do need a good18 minutes in there to make sure the sausages are nice and cooked.

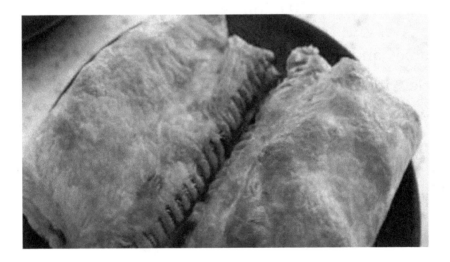

After the 18 minutes they're ready to eat.

50. Air Fryer French Fries

It will not get more classic than French fries; the normally accepted technique is fairly, dare I say, air tight, but I really do have one additional trick in shop! Last, dip them in honey mustard, hot ketchup, garlic aioli, or all 3 blended together, such as I did

Ingredients

- 1 lb. russet potatoes, peeled

- 1/2 tsp kosher salt

- 2 tsp vegetable oil

- 1 pinch cayenne pepper

Instructions

❖ Slice segments into sticks too around 3/8 inch-wide.

❖ Cover potatoes with water and let boil for 5 minutes to discharge excess starches.

❖ Drain and cover with boiling water with several inches (or put in a bowl of boiling water). Let sit for 10 minutes.

❖ Drain potatoes and move onto several paper towels. Transfer to a mixing bowl drizzle with oil, season with cayenne, and toss to coat.

❖ Stack potatoes in a dual layer in the fryer basket. Slide out basket and throw fries; keep frying until golden brown, about 10 minutes longer. Toss chips with salt in a mixing bowl.

51.Cheese on Toast

Ingredients:

- Bread

- Garlic butter

- cayenne pepper

Method:

I'm going to show you how to make a really quick and easy cheese on toast. How I make my cheese on toast is I get the bread and I put garlic butter on each side of the bread.

For me this is a very important step. I then grate quite a generous amount of cheese and then sprinkle it over the top. I will also add a little dash of cayenne pepper on top. Pop into my air fryer on the pizza button so that is for eight minutes at 160 degrees. Once the time is up, it comes out perfect every single time with a real nice crunchy piece of toast.

52. Tomato Pork Chops

It is a rather quick and easy recipe.

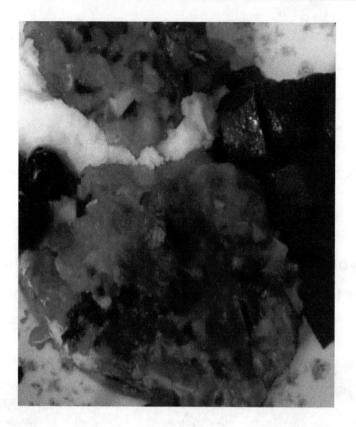

Ingredients

- 1 bell pepper - sliced, your color option

- 1 (15 oz.) can tomato sauce

- garlic powder to flavor

- 4 pork chops

- 1 tsp, sliced

- pepper and salt to taste

Directions

- ❖ Dredge the pork chops in flour, add to the pan and brown well on both sides.

❖ Add the onion and bell pepper, stir and cook for 5 minutes in the air fryer, or until nearly tender. Return pork chops to skillet and pour into the sauce. Permit the sauce to begin bubbling and reduce heat.

❖ Simmer for half an hour and season with garlic powder, pepper and salt to taste.

53. Veggie Egg Bread

Ingredients:

● 1 tsp salt

● ½ pound cream cheese

● 10 eggs

● 4 cups grated zucchini

● 1 cup grated cheddar cheese

● ½ cup chopped tomatoes

- ½ tsp ground black pepper

- ½ cup sliced mushrooms, cooked

- ½ cup almond flour

- 2 tsp baking powder

Directions

❖ Be sure the pan will fit on your air fryer- normally a seven inch round pan will do the job flawlessly.

❖ Stir together the almond milk, pepper, salt and baking powder.

❖ In another bowl, beat the cream cheese until its smooth and nice afterward insert the eggs. Beat until well blended.

❖ Add the zucchini into the cream cheese mixture and stir until incorporated.

❖ Add the dry mix to the cream cheese jar and then stir well.

❖ Pour into the prepared pan and then cook at the fryer for 45 minutes

54.**Easy Muffins**

Ingredients:

- Sugar

- Butter

- Flour

- Eggs

- Milk

- Salt

Method:

We're going to make cupcakes. I have got a hundred grams of sugar, 250 grams of butter, 250 grams of flour, 4 eggs, a splash of milk and a dash of salt. We're just going to whisk this all up. I have got some of these cupcake holders. They're silicon ones. I'm going to add it to those and then we'll put them into the air fryer on the cupcake setting and let them cook away.

55. Almond Flour Pancake

Ingredients:

- 1 teaspoon vanilla extract

- 1 1/4 cup almond milk

- two Tbsp. granulated erythritol

- 1 teaspoon baking powder

- 2 eggs

- 1/2 cup whole milk

- 2 Tbsp. butter, melted

- 1/8 tsp salt

Directions

- ❖ Be sure the pan will fit on your air fryer- normally a seven inch round pan will do the job flawlessly.

- ❖ Put the eggs, butter, milk and vanilla extract in a blender and puree for around thirty minutes.

- ❖ Add the remaining ingredients into the blender and puree until smooth.

- ❖ Pour the pancake batter to the prepared pan and set from the fryer.

- ❖ Cook for 2 minutes or until the pancake is puffed and the top is gold brown.

- ❖ Slice and serve with keto sugar free!

56. Zucchini and Bacon Egg Bread

Ingredients:

- ½ cup almond flour

- 1 tsp salt

- ½ pound cream cheese

- 10 eggs

- 2 tsp baking powder

- ½ tsp ground black pepper

- 1 pound bacon cooked and crumbled

- 4 cups grated zucchini

- 1 cup grated cheddar cheese

Directions

❖ Be sure the pan will fit on your air fryer- normally a seven inch round pan will do the job flawlessly.

❖ Stir together the almond milk, pepper, salt and baking powder.

❖ In another bowl, beat the cream cheese until its smooth and nice afterward insert the eggs. Beat until well blended.

❖ Add the zucchini into the cream cheese mixture and stir until incorporated.

❖ Add the dry mix to the cream cheese jar and then stir well.

❖ Pour into the prepared pan and then cook at the fryer for 45 minutes

57. Raspberry Almond Pancake

Ingredients:

- 1/2 cup whole milk

- 2 Tbsp. butter, melted

- 1 teaspoon almond extract

- 2 eggs

- two Tbsp. granulated erythritol

- 1 teaspoon baking powder

- 1/8 tsp salt

- 1 1/4 cup almond milk

- 1/4 cup frozen or fresh desserts

Directions

I. Preheat your air fryer to 420 degrees F and line a baking pan using parchment paper. Be sure the pan will fit on your air fryer- normally a seven inch round pan will do the job flawlessly.

II. Put the eggs, butter, milk and almond extract in a blender and puree for around thirty minutes.

III. Add the remaining ingredients into the blender and puree until smooth.

IV. Pour the pancake batter to the pan and stir in the raspberries

V. Lightly.

VI. Put in the fryer.

VII. Slice and serve with keto sugar free!

58. Maple Brussel Sprout Chips

Ingredients:

- 2 Tbsp. olive oil

- 1 tsp sea salt

- 1 Pound Brussel Sprouts, ends removed

- 1 tsp maple extract

Method:

➢ Preheat your air fryer to 2400 degrees F and line the fryer tray with parchment paper.

➢ Peel the Brussels sprouts leaf at a time, putting the leaves in a massive bowl as you pare them.

➢ Toss the leaves using the olive oil, maple extract and salt then disperse onto the prepared tray.

➢ Bake for 15 minutes at the fryer, tossing halfway through to cook evenly.

➢ Serve warm or wrap in an airtight container after chilled.

59. Sweet and Tangy Apple Pork Chops

That is a recipe that I made using the thought that apples and pork go beautifully together! The seasonings provide the pork a pleasant and slightly spicy flavor. The apple cider increases the sweetness, while still bringing an exceptional tartness, since it's absorbed into the meat. Serve with applesauce, if wanted. Hope you like it!

Ingredients:

- 3 tbsp. brown sugar

- 1/2 tsp garlic powder

- 2 tbsp. honey mustard

- 1 tsp mustard powder

- 1/2 teaspoon ground cumin

- 1 lb. pork chops

- 2 tbsp. butter

- 1/2 tsp cayenne pepper (Optional)

- 3/4 cup apple cider

Instructions

❑ Mix brown sugar, honey mustard, mustard powder, cumin, cayenne pepper, and garlic powder together in a small bowl. Rub pork chops and let sit on a plate for flavors to split into pork chops, about 10 minutes.

❑ Melt butter in a large skillet over moderate heat; include apple cider. Organize coated pork chops from the skillet;

❑ Cook until pork chops are browned, 5 to 7 minutes each side.

60. **Maple Brussel Sprout Chips**

Ingredients:

- 2 Tbsp. olive oil

- 1 tsp sea salt

- 1 Pound Brussel Sprouts, ends removed

- 1 tsp maple extract

Method:

➢ Preheat your air fryer to 2400 degrees F and line the fryer tray with parchment paper.

➢ Peel the Brussels sprouts leaf at a time, putting the leaves in a massive bowl as you pare them.

➢ Toss the leaves using the olive oil, maple extract and salt then disperse onto the prepared tray.

➢ Bake for 15 minutes at the fryer, tossing halfway through to cook evenly.

➢ Serve warm or wrap in an airtight container after chilled.

61.Blueberry Pancake

Ingredients:

- 2 Tbsp. butter, melted

- 1 teaspoon vanilla extract

- 1 1/4 cup almond milk

- 2 eggs

- 1 teaspoon baking powder

- 1/8 tsp salt

- 1/4 cup frozen or fresh blueberries

- 1/2 cup whole milk

- Two Tbsp. granulated erythritol

Directions

1. Preheat your air fryer to 400 degrees F and line a baking pan using parchment paper. Be sure the pan will fit on your fryer- normally a seven inch round pan will do the job flawlessly.

2. Put the eggs, butter, milk and vanilla extract in a blender and puree for around thirty minutes.

3. Add the remaining ingredients into the blender and puree until smooth.

4. Pour the pancake batter to the pan and stir in the blueberries

5. Put in the fryer.

6. Slice and serve with keto sugar free!

62. **Chocolate Croissants**

Ingredients

- Puff pastry

- Flake chocolate

Method:

I wanted to show you how to make some chocolate croissants in your air fryer as well. So, what I have got here is one roll of puff pastry and then to go on top to make it chocolatey, I have got some flake chocolate. What I'm going to do is roll out my puff pastry and then I'm going to crumble some flake chocolates all over the pastry.

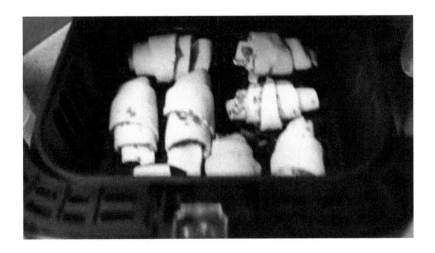

I'm then going to cut my pastry into eight. I'm going to cut them into fours and then I'll cut each four diagonally and then I'll roll them up into a croissant shape. Pop them into my air fryer, cook them on the muffin button which is a twelve minutes setting and then when they come out they are really really nice, chocolatey and delicious.

63. Strawberry Pancake

Ingredients:

- 1 teaspoon baking powder

- 1/8 tsp salt

- 1/4 cup fresh chopped tomatoes

- 2 eggs

- 1 teaspoon vanilla extract

- 1 1/4 cup almond milk

Directions

I. Pre-heat the air fryer for around 15 minutes.

II. Put the eggs, butter, milk and vanilla extract in a blender and simmer for about half an hour.

III. Add the remaining ingredients into the blender and puree until smooth.

IV. Pour the pancake batter to the pan and stir in the berries gently.

V. Put in the fryer.

VI. Slice and serve with keto sugar free!

64. Cheesy Zucchini Bake

Ingredients:

- 2 tsp baking powder

- ½ tsp ground black pepper

- 1 tsp salt

- ½ cup almond flour

- 4 cups grated zucchini

- ½ pound cream cheese

- 10 eggs

- 1 cup grated cheddar cheese

Method:

1. Be sure the pan will fit on your air fryer- normally a seven inch round pan will do the job flawlessly. If it's possible to fit a bigger pan, then do so!

2. Stir together the almond milk, pepper, salt and baking powder.

3. In another bowl beat the cream cheese until its smooth and nice afterward insert the eggs. Beat until well blended.

4. Add the zucchini into the cream cheese mixture and stir until incorporated.

5. Add the dry mix to the cream cheese jar and then stir well.

6. Pour into the prepared pan and then cook at the fryer for 45 minutes.

65. Basil-Garlic Grilled Pork Chops

I had been tired of the exact same old agendas, and opted to try out something new... WOW! These chops are excellent!! They're fantastic for casual entertaining or family dinner. Together with the fresh basil and grated garlic, the taste is quite refreshing! Everybody will adore these!

Ingredients

- 4 (8 ounce) pork chops

- 4 cloves garlic, minced

- ¼ cup chopped fresh basil

- 1 lime, juiced

- salt and black pepper to taste

Instructions

❖ Toss the pork chops with all the carrot juice in a bowl until evenly coated. Toss with ginger and garlic. Season the chops to taste with pepper and salt. Set aside to marinate for half an hour.

❖ Cook the pork chops on the fryer till no longer pink at the middle, 5 to 10 minutes each side.

66. Full English breakfast

Full English breakfast is one that my family really really likes. We have lived in England for a while so my kids really look forward to Saturday morning so that we make full English breakfast. However today I'm going to be showing you a special way to make it stress free.

I'm going to be starting off with the hash browns.

Ingredients:

- Potatoes

- Cheese

- Egg

- Salt

- Pepper

- Chili Flakes

- Sausage

Method:

So, the hash brownies are going to be composed of potatoes. I'm going to be using two, then I'm also going to be using cheese. This is shredded cheese and this is like the equivalent of one and a half cups of cheese. We are also going to be using one egg, this is one raw egg and some all-purpose flour, and this is the equivalent of two huge teaspoons of flour. We will be using some pepper along with chili flakes and finally of course some salt to taste. Right, so these are the ingredients that I'm going to be using for the hash browns.

Before we start off with hash browns let's move on to all the other ingredients or condiments that are going to make up the English breakfast so part of the traditional ones we also use would be the eggs so this will make up we're going to make sunny side up eggs I'm going to be using some tomatoes some sausage, so this is not this is not the same way you have a traditional English breakfast.

This isn't the same kind of way the sausage is or the way to slice but this is fine. Then we're going to be including baked beans right. So, this is a shop bought and actually there's still one more ingredient I'm going to be using: bacon. This is raw thinly sliced bacon and we have two slices of bread right. So, that's all the components or the condiments are going to go into the full English breakfast.

Let's start off straight away with the hash browns because all these other things are pretty much ready to go. Let's start with the preparation of the hash browns. So the first thing I'm going to be doing to grate the potatoes. With grated you can use any size. I want to use the really thin size because I want it more or less almost if it's already mashed or boiled. Because I'm going to be putting it in an array, I want it to take as little time as possible in order to get the potatoes done. If you've had English breakfast before let me know what you include or what you remove. I know people have different types of English breakfast at different times. Yeah, I know there's the black pudding, if you're a traditional English person you probably like black pudding instead.

We're done with the grating of the potatoes and I've rinsed it out in sense that I've put some water in. I'm giving it a good squeeze to make sure all the water is gone. This helps to remove the majority of the starch in the potatoes. So it's completely up to you, if you want to skip this process in the sense that you want to rinse out some of the water from the potatoes. Okay so that done, the next thing we're going to move on to the mixing. I'm going to put in my flour. This is two teaspoons but it seems like I'm going to use only one. Then I remember eggs, had a full raw egg for my potato to make the hash browns. I also have some cheese, add some salt to taste and some chili flakes. I like something hot and spicy and yeah that's why I add that. So, I give this a really good mix for hash browns, people usually sometimes add butter so it's completely up to you what you want to include in your own hash browns. I'm just keeping my own soft shots sweet and simple. You can add or subtract as much as you want.

I'm going to give my tray a spray just to oil it, because what I'm going to do guys, this is something different. I'm going to start off with the hash browns. I'm putting everything and it's going to come out like a cup sort of like a cupcake, because my cans are a bit deep. I'm going to spread it into two sections right because I want it to cook all the way through so the potatoes are going to come out, sort of like a cupcake or potato cups. I'm also going to give this another spray right now, this is different.

I'm going to put in oops my sausages right, to line them all in here. As I'm using the air fryer for everything stress less so hopefully this should work for a bachelor or spencer or a small family or just making breakfast for somebody for just one person in the family. This works pretty good. I'm going to put them in first so the next thing that is going to be included in the air fryer all three of them are going in now is the bacon. I'm going to put the bacon this way, alternatively, I could have chopped up the bacon and put them in one of these sections. Maybe I would actually just do that so that you have a look-see at its rest of the bacon. I'm just going to cut this one in here.

Throw it into the extra bit there again, I'm not going to be bothered about these bacon, because you know they're going to come up with their own oil. It's going to go into the air fryer oven. Put it in the air fryer oven and let it fry just turning the timer to one hour. It's an air fryer oven and the specific degree setting should be up on your screen and yeah so once this is ready again, like I said it's halfway into the cooking of the sausages of the hash browns and the bacon.

I'm now going to include the baked beans and the eggs because those ones will actually take less time compared to what you've got in the oven. I've had these in the air fryer and I can see that my bacon is coming out nicely.

You see that so it depends on you if this is how you like your bacons this is the point in which you take them out. So, I'm just going to chuck the monotone section of the cupcake bits. What I'm going to do is to put the ones that are under done on the top and the ones that are already getting as crisp, I'm going to put them at the bottom. Now I'm just trying to get my stuff together. I'm scooping out all the sausages tone section so that I have two sections free for me to put my eggs and my baked beans. I'm going to have the egg sunny side up, I'm not going to spray the container again because all the bacon oil is in the egg, is in the cupcake holder. I'm just going to break two eggs and putting two into one section and then add some salt and some chili flakes. Our egg begins to cool, then I'm also going to put in the baked beans right in the final section. We are all good to go so I just want to show you guys what it looks like.

We've got the eggs we've got the baked beans we've got everything in the section in the containers. I'm going to have the the tomatoes, I'm just going to line them on top here and yeah voila. I know for some people it's a lot of work but this is really stress less. The only bit where you have lots of work to do is with the grating of the potatoes and that's pretty much it. We're going to allow these now to cook all the way through by the time the egg is done and the baked paint is ready, the entire dish should be ready. We're about 30 minutes into the entire thing and it's looking really really good. I just want to bring this and mix up the sausages a bit, yeah and put this back because you need a couple of minutes to go. You can see the egg, you can see the bacon everything is looking wonderful. I'm going to move this all the way back because I want to put my tomatoes just to give it a little bit of somehow grilled max and then my bread right just to heat it up.

Let it give me somewhat like a mini toast. I'm going to shut this down now its done 30 minutes and it's done right. I'm not looking to get toasted bread but I just want this really warm. It's not toasted but it's warm and really crispy. I'm going to get the bread out of the way and the same thing with the tomatoes. So they're just warm so that when the breakfast is being eaten it's really nice and warm and fuzzy. Let's get onto plating it okay we are all ready, can you see that looks really good so and this is every single thing in one place right. So, our potatoes looks properly cooked a bit hot, our hash browns potatoes looks good and you can see our sausages. It did really really well cooked properly right and the same thing with the bacon so you can see all crispy or crunchy. I was able to achieve breakfast.

It took me about 30 minutes to make the entire dish so you can see my eggs yummy yummy yummy. I'm just going to dish this out and yeah so you can see the entire dish all presented for you. This is our English breakfast right you have the bread, we've got the bacon, I'm going to put in the sausages. This is a wonderful breakfast. All I really did was just to check it up at various times and baked beans is ready. This could actually is pretty decent meal and I think can it's perfect for more than one person. We have got egg there's not mushroom, there is no black pudding but this is completely fine the way it is right. So, this is what our full English breakfast looks like on some days and I've got the eggs, I've got the bacon, I still have some bacon there in the tray because I did make a lot so, still have some eggs.

 I have got some bacon some bread, yeah with a glass of milk or a cup of coffee you're good to go.

67. Garlic Brussel Sprout Chips

Ingredients:

- 1 tsp sea salt

- 1 Pound Brussel Sprouts, ends removed

- 2 Tbsp. olive oil

- 1 tsp garlic powder

Method:

❖ Preheat your air fryer to 2400 degrees F and line the fryer tray with parchment paper.

❖ Peel the Brussels sprouts leaf at a time, putting the leaves in a massive bowl as you pare them.

❖ Toss the leaves together with olive oil, garlic powder and salt then disperse onto the prepared tray.

❖ Bake for 15 minutes at the fryer, tossing halfway through to cook evenly.

68. Home and Asparagus

Ingredients:

- 1/4 teaspoon ground black pepper

- 1/4 tsp salt

- 1 lb. asparagus spears

Directions

- ❏ Preheat your air fryer to 400 degrees F and line your fryer tray using a

- ❏ Set the cod filets onto the parchment and sprinkle with the pepper and salt and rub the spices to the fish.

- ❏ Top the fish with the remaining components then wrap the parchment paper around the fish filets, surrounding them entirely.

- ❏ Put the tray in the fryer and bake for 20 minutes.

69. Herbed Parmesan Crackers

Ingredients:

- 2 Tbsp. Italian seasoning

- ½ cup chia seeds

- 1 ½ cups sunflower seeds

- 1 egg

- 2 Tbsp. butter, melted

- Salt

- ½ tsp garlic powder

- ½ tsp baking powder

- ¾ cup parmesan cheese, grated

Method:

❑ Set the sunflower seeds and chia seeds in a food processor until finely mixed to a powder. Put into a large bowl.

❑ Add the cheese, Italian seasoning, garlic powder and baking powder to the bowl and combine well.

❑ Add the melted butter and egg and stir till a wonderful dough forms.

❑ Put the dough onto a sheet of parchment and then put the following slice of parchment on top.

❑ Roll the dough into a thin sheet around 1/8 inch thick.

❑ Remove the top piece of parchment and lift the dough with the underside parchment and set onto a sheet tray which can fit in the air fryer.

❑ Score the cracker dough to your desired shape and bake for 40-45cminutes.

❑ Break the crackers aside and enjoy!

70. Salmon and Asparagus

Ingredients:

- ¼ tsp ground black pepper

- 1 ¾ pound salmon fillets

- ¼ tsp salt

- 1 pound asparagus spears

- 1 Tbsp. lemon juice

- 1 Tbsp. fresh chopped parsley

- 3 Tbsp. olive oil

Method

→ Preheat your air fryer to 400 degrees F and line your fryer tray using a long piece of parchment paper.

→ Set the salmon filets onto the parchment and sprinkle with the salt and pepper and rub the spices to the fish.

→ Top the fish with the rest of the ingredients then wrap the parchment paper around the fish filets, surrounding them completely.

→ Put the tray in the fryer and bake for 20 minutes.

71. Super Seed Parmesan Crackers

Ingredients:

- ½ tsp baking powder

- 1 egg

- 2 Tbsp. butter, melted

- 1 cups sunflower seeds

- ¾ cup parmesan cheese, grated

- 2 Tbsp. Italian seasoning

- ½ cup chia seeds

- ½ cup hulled hemp seeds

- ½ tsp garlic powder

- Salt

Method:

★ Preheat your air fryer to 300 degrees F.

★ Put into a large bowl.

★ Add the cheese, Italian seasoning, garlic powder and baking powder to the bowl and combine well.

★ Add the melted butter and egg and stir till a wonderful dough forms.

★ Put the dough onto a sheet of parchment and then put the following slice of parchment on top.

★ Roll the dough into a thin sheet around 1/8 inch thick.

★ Remove the top piece of parchment and lift the dough with the underside parchment and set onto a sheet tray which will fit from the air fryer.

★ Score the cracker dough to your desired shape and bake for 40-45 minutes.

★ Break the crackers aside and enjoy!

Conclusion

We have included 70 best recipes for you in this book. So, just try it out and then give us feedback with images of cooking.

Keto Air Fryer Cookbook

Cook and Taste Tens of Low-Carb Fried Recipes. Shed Weight, Kill Hunger, and Regain Confidence Living the Keto Lifestyle

By

Giovanni Paletto

Contents

Introduction

An air-fryer is a modern kitchen device that cooks food instead of using oil by blowing extremely hot air around it. It provides a low-fat variant of food that in a deep fryer will usually be fried. Consequently, fatty foods such as French fries, fried chicken, and onion rings are usually prepared with no oil or up to 80% less fat relative to traditional cooking techniques.

If you already have an air fryer, you probably know that it's a futuristic gadget designed to save time and help make your life easier. You'll be eager to hear about how soon you'll be addicted to using your air fryer for cooking almost any meal if you've still not taken the jump. What is so unique about air frying, though?

The air fryer will substitute your deep fryer, microwave, oven, and dehydrator and cook tasty meals uniformly in a very small amount of time. Your air fryer is a show stopper if you're trying to help your friends with nutritious food but do not have much time.

With your progress on the ketogenic diet, an air fryer will also aid. The fast cooking time it offers is one of the main advantages of air frying. When you are starving and limited on resources, this is extremely helpful, a formula for cheating on your keto diet. Simple planning of nutritious meals is also linked to long-term progress on a keto diet. That's why during your keto trip, your air fryer can be your best buddy and support you to stay on track, even on days when time is limited for you.

The Air Fryer offers fried foods and nutritious meals, helping you eliminate the calories that come with fried foods and providing you the crunchiness, taste, and flavor you love. By blowing very hot air (up to 400 ° F) uniformly and rapidly around a food ingredient put in an enclosed room, this household appliance works. The heat renders the food part on the outside crispy and brittle, but it is warm and moist on the inside. You can use an air fryer on pretty much everything. You should barbecue, bake and roast in addition to frying. Its choice of cooking choices allows it simpler at any time of the day to eat any food.

Cooking using an Air Fryer

It is as simple to cook with an air fryer as using an oven. Anyone may do it, and then you'll wish that you had turned to this brilliant cooking process earlier after only a few tries. This section will outline air frying choices, optimize your cooking period and juiciness, clarify how to make your air fryer clean and offer some gadgets that will make sure that your air frying experience is even simpler and more pleasant.

Although the fundamentals of using an air fryer would be discussed in this section, the first phase is studying the guide that comes along with the air fryer. Almost all air fryers are distinct, and there are several different versions of the industry with the recent spike in device demand. Knowing how to thoroughly operate your particular air fryer is the secret to victory and can familiarize you with debugging concerns as well as protection features. Until first use, reading through the guide and washing every component with soft, soapy water can make you feel prepared to release your cooking finesse!

Why Use It:

Air frying is widely common because it enables you to cook tasty meals easily and uniformly with very small quantity of oil and very little energy. Here are only a handful of reasons to turn to air frying:

Quick cleanup: You would certainly stain your cooker with every cooking process, but with the smaller frying region of the air fryer and portable basket, comprehensive cleanup is a breeze!

Cooks faster: By rotating heated air throughout the cooking compartment, air frying operates. This contributes to quick and even frying, using a portion of your oven's resources. You can set most air fryers to an extreme temperature of around 350-400°F. Because of which, in an air fryer, you can cook just about everything you can create in a microwave.

Low-Fat Food: The most important feature of the air fryer is the usage of hot-air airflow to cook food products from all directions, removing the need for gasoline. This makes it easier for individuals on a reduced-fat diet to eat deliciously balanced meals safely.

Highly Safe: While tossing chicken or any other ingredients into the deep fryer, do you know how extra cautious you have to be? As it is still really hot, you want to be sure that the hot oil does not spill and damage your face. You wouldn't have to think about brunette skin from hot oil spillage with your air fryer.

Multifunctional Use: Since it can cook many dishes at once, the air fryer helps you multitask. It is your all-in-one gadget that can barbecue, bake, fry and roast the dishes you need! For separate work, you no longer require several appliances.

Healthier Foods: Air fryers are built to operate without fattening oils and up to 80 percent less fat to create healthier foods. This makes it possible to lose weight because you can also enjoy your fried dishes while retaining calories and saturated fat. Through utilizing this appliance, making the transition to a healthy existence is more feasible. The scent that comes with deep-fried items, which also hangs in the room even many hours after deep frying, is also eliminated from your house.

Selecting a Custom Air Fryer:

The dual most significant aspects to concentrate on are scale/size and heat range when picking an air fryer. In general, quart scale air fryers are calculated and vary from around 1.2 quarts size to about 10 quarts or even more. You may be drawn in at a minimum a 5.3-quart fryer which may be used to wonderfully roast a whole chicken if you are trying to prepare meals to serve a group, but if you require a tiny machine owing to the minimal counter room and you are preparing for just one or two, you can certainly crisp up those Fries with a much minor air fryer.

And for the range of temperatures available, many air fryers encourage you to dry out foods and, for a prolonged period, you can fry them at extremely low heat, say about 120 ° F. You'll want to ensure the air fryer takes the necessary cooking power and heat range, based on the functions you use.

Accessories

The cooking chamber of your air fryer is essentially just a wide, open room for the warm air to move. It is a big bonus because it offers you the opportunity to integrate into your kitchen some different accessories. These devices increase the amount of dishes that you can produce using your air fryer and start opening choices that you might never have known was feasible. Below are few of the popular gadgets.

Parchment: In specific, precut parchment may be useful while baking with your air fryer to make cleaning much simpler. Similarly, for quick steaming, you will find parchment paper with precut holes.

Pizza pan: Indeed, using the air fryer, you can make a pizza, and this book contains many recipes for various kinds of keto-friendly pizzas. This is a fantastic alternative to still have the desired form quickly.

Cupcake pan: It typically comes with several tiny cups, and the 5.3-quart size air fryer takes up the whole chamber. For cupcakes, muffins, or even egg plates, these flexible cups are fine. You can still use single silicone baking containers if you would not want to go this path.

Cake pan: For your air fryer, you will find specially designed cake pans that fit perfectly into the inner pot. They even come with a built-in handle so that when your cakes are finished baking, you can quickly take them out.

Skewer rack: This is identical to a holder made of aluminum, except it has built-in skewers of metal that make roasting kebabs a breeze.

Metal holder: To add a layer to your cooking plate, this round rack is used so that you can optimize room and cook several items simultaneously. When you cook meat and vegetables and don't want to stop to cook to get going on the other, this is especially helpful.

How to clean an Air Fryer

Make sure that the air fryer is cold and unhooked before washing it. To wash the air fryer slate, you'll need to follow the steps below:

1. Separate your air fryer plate from its foundation. Fill a tub of worm water and soap for your pan. Let the plate sit in warm water and soap mix for about 10 minutes with your frying bucket inside.

2. Using a brush or sponge, thoroughly clean the bucket.

3. Lift the basket from the frying pan and clean the underneath and exterior surfaces.

4. Now use the same brush or sponge to clean your air-fryer plate.

5. Allow all to air-dry completely and transfer to the foundation of the air fryer.

Simply scrub the exterior with a wet cloth to disinfect the exterior of your air fryer. Then, before starting your next cooking experience, make sure all parts are in there right places.

Keto Diet

A relatively moderate-protein, low-carb, and elevated diet that help the body sustain itself without using sugars or high amounts of carbs is the keto diet or keto. When the system is low on glucose (sugar), ketones are formed by a mechanism called ketosis in the liver from food metabolism. This diet will contribute to some lower blood sugar, weight loss, balanced insulin levels, plus managed cravings, with diligent monitoring, imaginative meals, and self-control.

Your body takes some carbohydrates as you consume high-carb nutrition and converts them into energy to fuel itself. Your liver instead burns fat as you leave out the carbohydrates. A ketogenic régime usually limits carbohydrates to about 0-50 grams a day.

Tips for Usage:
- Preheat your fryer before use
- Always cook in batches. Do not overcrowd your fryer

- Space Your Foods evenly when added to the air fryer
- Keep It Dry
- Use spray oil to oil your food

CHAPTER 1: Breakfast Recipes

If you set your air fryer to work, simple and healthy low-carb breakfasts will soon be the rule in your home! These meals will boot the day in a nutritious way without robbing you of days that should be full of savory fun! It can be not easy to make a nourishing meal for oneself or relatives while you're trying to get out of the house in time. The easiest choice might be to catch a granola bar or microwave pastry, but it will quickly contribute to thoughts of shame and guilt and extreme malnutrition at noon.

This section's meals are full and keto-approved, making you improve your mornings and all your days. Get prepared in a snap for nutritious meals that can be created using your air fryer. You can make meals in advance, such as Cheese Balls, and Sausage and you can put dishes in the air fryer to get ready until you get dressed, such as Quick and Simple Bacon Strips, you'll want to have begun frying your breakfasts earlier!

1. Loaded Cauliflower Breakfast Bake

Preparation time: 15 minutes

Cooking time: 20 minutes

Servings: 4 people

Ingredients:

- 12 slices sugar-free bacon, cooked and crumbled
- 2 scallions, sliced on the bias
- 8 tablespoons full-fat sour cream
- 1 medium avocado, peeled and pitted
- 1 cup shredded medium Cheddar cheese
- 11/2 cups chopped cauliflower
- 1/4 cup heavy whipping cream
- 6 large eggs

Directions:

1. Mix the eggs and milk in a medium dish. Pour it into a circular 4-cup baking tray.

2. Add and blend the cauliflower, and cover it with cheddar. Put your dish in the air-fryer bowl.

3. Change the temperature and set the timer to about 320°F for around 20 minutes.

4. The eggs will be solid once fully baked, and the cheese will be golden brown. Slice it into 4 bits.

5. Cut the avocado and split the bits equally. Put two teaspoons of sliced scallions, sour cream, and crumbled bacon on top of each plate.

2. Scrambled Eggs

Preparation time: 5 minutes

Cooking time: 20 minutes

Servings: 2 people

Ingredients:

- 1/2 cup shredded sharp Cheddar cheese
- 2 tablespoons unsalted butter, melted
- 4 large eggs

Directions:

1. Crack the eggs into a round 2-cup baking pan and whisk them. Put the tray in the air-fryer container.

2. Change the temperature settings and set the timer to about 400°F for around 10 minutes.

3. Mix the eggs after about 5 minutes and add some cheese and butter. Let it cook for another 3 minutes and mix again.

4. Give an extra 2 minutes to finish frying or remove the eggs from flame if they are to your preferred taste.

5. For fluffing, use a fork. Serve it hot.

3. "Hard-Boiled" Eggs

Preparation time: 2 minutes

Cooking time: 20 minutes

Servings: 4 people

Ingredients:

- 1 cup water
- 4 large eggs

Directions:

1. Put the eggs in a heat-proof 4-cup round baking tray and pour some water over your eggs. Put the tray in the air-fryer basket.

2. Set the air fryer's temperature to about 300 ° F and set the clock for about 18-minute.

3. In the fridge, store boiled eggs before ready to consume or peel and serve warmly.

4. Breakfast Stuffed Poblanos

Preparation time: 20 minutes

Cooking time: 15 minutes

Servings: 5 people

Ingredients:

- 1/2 cup full-fat sour cream
- 8 tablespoons shredded pepper jack cheese
- 4 large poblano peppers
- 1/4 cup canned diced tomatoes and green chilies, drained
- 4 ounces full-fat cream cheese, softened
- 4 large eggs
- 1/2 pound spicy ground pork breakfast sausage

Directions:

1. Crumble and brown the cooked sausage in a large skillet over medium-low heat until no red exists. Take the sausage from the skillet and clean the oil. Crack your eggs in the skillet, scramble, and simmer until they are no longer watery.

2. In a wide bowl, add the fried sausage and add in cream cheese. Mix the sliced tomatoes and chilies. Gently fold the eggs together.

3. Cut a 4-5-inch gap at the top of each poblano, separating the white layer and seeds with a tiny knife. In four portions, divide the filling and gently scoop into each pepper. Cover each with 2 teaspoons of cheese from the pepper jack.

4. Drop each pepper into the container of the air fryer.

5. Change the temperature and set the timer to about 350 °F for around 15 minutes.

6. The peppers will be tender, and when prepared, the cheese will be golden brown. Serve instantly with sour cream on top.

5. Cheesy Cauliflower Hash Browns

Preparation time: 20 minutes

Cooking time: 12 minutes

Servings: 4 people

Ingredients:

- 1 cup shredded sharp Cheddar cheese
- 1 large egg
- 1 (12-ounce) steamer bag cauliflower

Directions:

1. Put the bag in the oven and cook as per the directions in the box. To extract excess moisture, leave to cool fully and place cauliflower in a cheesecloth or paper towel and squeeze.

2. Add the cheese and eggs and mash the cauliflower using a fork.

3. Cut a slice of parchment to match the frame of your air fryer. Take 1/4 of the paste and make it into a hash-brown patty shape and mold it. Put it on the parchment and, into your air fryer basket, if required, running in groups.

4. Change the temperature and set the clock to about 400°F for around 12 minutes.

5. Halfway into the cooking process, turn your hash browns. They will be nicely browned when fully baked. Instantly serve.

6. Egg, Cheese, and Bacon Roll-Ups

Preparation time: 20 minutes

Cooking time: 20 minutes

Servings: 4 people

Ingredients:

- 1/2 cup mild salsa for dipping

- 1 cup shredded sharp Cheddar cheese

- 12 slices sugar free bacon

- 6 large eggs

- 1/2 medium green bell pepper, seeded and chopped

- 1/4 cup chopped onion

- 2 tablespoons unsalted butter

Directions:

1. Melt the butter in a small skillet over medium flame. Add the pepper and onion to the skillet and sauté until aromatic, around 3 minutes, and your onions are transparent.

2. In a shallow pot, whisk the eggs and dump them into a skillet. Scramble the pepper and onion with the eggs once fluffy and fully fried after 5 minutes. Remove from the flame and set aside.

3. Put 3 strips of bacon beside each other on the cutting board, overlapping about 1/4. Place 1/4 cup of scrambled eggs on the side nearest to you in a pile and scatter 1/4 cup of cheese on top of your eggs.

4. Wrap the bacon around the eggs securely and, if needed, protect the seam using a toothpick. Put each wrap into the container of the air fryer.

5. Switch the temperature to about 350 ° F and set the clock for around 15 minutes. Midway through the cooking time, turn the rolls.

6. When fully fried, the bacon would be brown and tender. For frying, serve immediately with some salsa.

7. Pancake

Preparation time: 10 minutes

Cooking time: 7 minutes

Servings: 4 people

Ingredients:

- 1/2 teaspoon ground cinnamon
- 1/2 teaspoon vanilla extract
- 1/2 teaspoon unflavored gelatin
- 1 large egg
- 2 tablespoons unsalted butter, softened
- 1/2 teaspoon baking powder
- 1/4 cup powdered erythritol
- 1/2 cup blanched finely ground almond flour

Directions:

1. Combine the erythritol, almond flour, and baking powder in a wide pot. Add some egg, butter, cinnamon, gelatin, and vanilla. Place into a rectangular 6-inch baking tray.

2. Place the tray in the container of your air fryer.

3. Change the temperature to about 300 °F and set the clock for 7 minutes.

4. A toothpick can pop out dry when the dessert is fully baked. Split the cake into four servings and eat.

8. Lemon Poppy Seed Cake

Preparation time: 10 minutes

Cooking time: 14 minutes

Servings: 6 people

Ingredients:

- 1 teaspoon poppy seeds
- 1 medium lemon
- 1 teaspoon vanilla extract
- 2 large eggs
- 1/4 cup unsweetened almond milk
- 1/4 cup unsalted butter, melted
- 1/2 teaspoon baking powder
- 1/2 cup powdered erythritol
- 1 cup blanched finely ground almond flour

Directions:

Mix the erythritol, almond flour, butter, baking powder, eggs, almond milk, and vanilla in a big bowl.

Halve the lime and strain the liquid into a little pot, then transfer it to the mixture.

Zest the lemon with a fine grinder and transfer 1 tbsp. of zest to the mixture and blend. Add the poppy seeds to your batter.

In the non-stick 6' circular cake tin, add your batter. Put the pan in the container of your air fryer.

Change the temperature and set the clock to about 300°F for around 14 minutes.

A wooden skewer inserted in the middle, if it comes out completely clean, means it's thoroughly fried. The cake will stop cooking and crisp up when it cools. At room temperature, serve.

9. "Banana" Nut Cake

Preparation time: 20 minutes

Cooking time: 30 minutes

Servings: 6-7 people

Ingredients:

- 1/4 cup of chopped walnuts
- 2 large eggs
- 1/4 cup of full-fat sour cream
- 1 teaspoon of vanilla extract
- 21/2 teaspoons of banana extract
- 1/4 cup of unsalted butter, melted
- 1/2 teaspoon of ground cinnamon
- 2 teaspoons of baking powder
- 2 tablespoons of ground golden flaxseed
- 1/2 cup of powdered erythritol
- 1 cup of blanched finely ground almond flour

Directions:

1. Mix the erythritol, almond flour, baking powder, flaxseed, and cinnamon in a big dish.

2. Add vanilla extract, banana extract, butter, and sour cream and mix well.

3. Add your eggs to the combination and whisk until they are fully mixed. Mix in your walnuts.

4. Pour into a 6-inch non-stick cake pan and put in the bowl of your air fryer.

5. Change the temperature and set the clock to about 300°F for around 25 minutes.

6. When fully baked, the cake will be lightly golden, and a toothpick inserted in the middle will come out clean. To prevent cracking, allow it to cool entirely.

10. Bacon Strips

Preparation time: 5 minutes

Cooking time: 12 minutes

Servings: 5 people

Ingredients:

- 10 slices sugar free bacon

Directions:

1. Put slices of bacon into the bucket of your air fryer.

2. Change the temperature and set the timer to about 400°F for around 12 minutes.

3. Turn the bacon after 6 minutes and proceed to cook. Serve hot.

11.Pumpkin Spice Muffins

Preparation time: 10 minutes

Cooking time: 15 minutes

Servings: 6 people

Ingredients:

- 2 large eggs

- 1 teaspoon vanilla extract

- 1/4 teaspoon ground nutmeg

- 1/2 teaspoon ground cinnamon

- 1/4 cup pure pumpkin purée

- 1/4 cup unsalted butter, softened

- 1/2 teaspoon baking powder

- 1/2 cup granular erythritol

- 1 cup blanched finely ground almond flour

Directions:

1. Mix the erythritol, almond flour, butter, baking powder, nutmeg, cinnamon, pumpkin purée, and vanilla in a big dish.

2. Stir in the eggs softly.

3. Add the batter into about six or more silicone muffin cups equally. Put muffin cups in the air fryer basket. If required, make them in groups.

4. Change the temperature and set the clock to about 300°F for around 15 minutes.

5. A wooden skewer inserted in the middle will come out completely clean if thoroughly cooked. Serve hot.

12. Veggie Frittata

Preparation time: minutes

Cooking time: minutes

Servings: people

Ingredients:

- 1/4 cup of chopped green bell pepper
- 1/4 cup of chopped yellow onion
- 1/2 cup of chopped broccoli
- 1/4 cup of heavy whipping cream
- 6 large eggs

Directions:

1. Whisk the heavy whipping cream and eggs in a big bowl. Add in the onion, broccoli, and bell pepper.

2. Load into a 6-inch circular baking dish that is oven-safe. Put the baking tray in the basket of an air fryer.

3. Switch the temperature to about 350 ° F and set the clock for around 12-minute.

4. When the frittata is finished, eggs must be solid and thoroughly cooked. Serve it hot.

13. Buffalo Egg Cups

Preparation time: 12 minutes

Cooking time: 12 minutes

Servings: 3 people

Ingredients:

- 1/2 cup of shredded sharp Cheddar cheese
- 2 tablespoons of buffalo sauce
- 2 ounces of full-fat cream cheese
- 4 large eggs

Directions:

1. In two (4') ramekins, add the eggs.

2. Mix the buffalo sauce, cream cheese, and cheddar in a little, microwave-safe container. For about 20 seconds, microwave and then mix. Put a spoonful on top of each egg within each ramekin.

3. Put the ramekins in the container of an air fryer.

4. Change the temperature and set the timer to about 320°F for around 15 minutes.

5. Serve it hot.

14. Crispy Southwestern Ham Egg Cups

Preparation time: 5 minutes

Cooking time: 14 minutes

Servings: 3 people

Ingredients:

- 1/2 cup of shredded medium Cheddar cheese
- 2 tablespoons of diced white onion
- 2 tablespoons of diced red bell pepper
- 1/4 cup diced of green bell pepper
- 2 tablespoons of full-fat sour cream
- 4 large eggs
- 4 (1-ounce) of slices deli ham

Directions:

1. Put a piece of ham at the bottom of four or more baking cups.
2. Whisk the eggs along with the sour cream in a big bowl. Add the red pepper, green pepper, and onion and mix well.
3. Add the mixture of eggs into baking cups that are ham-lined. Top them with some cheddar cheese. Put the cups in the container of your air fryer.
4. Set the clock for around 12 minutes or till the peaks are golden browned, cook at a temperature of about 320 ° F.
5. Serve it hot.

15. Jalapeño Popper Egg Cups

Preparation time: 10 minutes

Cooking time: 12 minutes

Servings: 3 people

Ingredients:

- 1/2 cup of shredded sharp Cheddar cheese
- 2 ounces of full-fat cream cheese
- 1/4 cup of chopped pickled jalapeños
- 4 large eggs

Directions:

1. Add the eggs to a medium container, and then dump them into 4 silicone muffin cups.

2. Place the cream cheese, jalapeños, and cheddar in a wide, microwave-safe dish. Heat in the microwave for about 30 seconds and mix well. Take a full spoon and put it in the middle of one of the egg cups, around 1/4 of the paste. Repeat for the mixture left.

3. Put the egg cups in the container of your air fryer.

4. Change the temperature and set the clock for around 10 minutes to about 320 °F.

5. Serve it hot.

16. Crunchy Granola

Preparation time: 10 minutes

Cooking time: 5 minutes

Servings: 6 people

Ingredients:

- 1 teaspoon of ground cinnamon
- 2 tablespoons of unsalted butter
- 1/4 cup of granular erythritol
- 1/4 cup of low-carb, sugar free chocolate chips
- 1/4 cup of golden flaxseed
- 1/3 cup of sunflower seeds
- 1 cup of almond slivers
- 1 cup of unsweetened coconut flakes
- 2 cups of pecans, chopped

Directions:

1. Blend all the ingredients in a big bowl.

2. In a 4-cup circular baking tray, put the mixture into it.

3. Place the tray in the air-fryer container.

4. Change the temperature and set the clock to about 320°F for around 5 minutes.

5. Let it cool absolutely before serving.

CHAPTER 2: Air Fryer Chicken Main Dishes

1. Chicken Fajitas

Preparation time: 10 minutes

Cooking time: 15 minutes

Servings: 2 people

Ingredients:

- 1/2 medium red bell pepper, seeded and sliced
- 1/2 medium green bell pepper, seeded and sliced
- 1/4 medium onion, peeled and sliced
- 1/2 teaspoon garlic powder
- 1/2 teaspoon paprika
- 1/2 teaspoon cumin
- 1 tablespoon chili powder
- 2 tablespoons coconut oil, melted
- 10 ounces boneless, skinless chicken breast, sliced into 1/4" strips

Directions:

1. In a big bowl, mix the chicken and coconut oil and scatter with the paprika, cumin, chili powder, and garlic powder. Toss the chicken with spices until well mixed. Put the chicken in the basket of an air fryer.

2. Set the temperature and adjust the clock to about 350°F for around 15 minutes.

3. When your clock has 7 minutes left, throw in the peppers and onion into the fryer bucket.

4. When frying, flip the chicken at least two to three times. Veggies should be soft; when done, the chicken should be thoroughly cooked to at least 165°F internal temperature. Serve it hot.

2. Pepperoni and Chicken Pizza Bake

Preparation time: 10 minutes

Cooking time: 15 minutes

Servings: 4 people

Ingredients:

- 1/4 cup grated Parmesan cheese
- 1 cup shredded mozzarella cheese
- 1 cup low-carb, sugar-free pizza sauce
- 20 slices pepperoni
- 2 cups cubed cooked chicken

Directions:

1. Add the pepperoni, chicken, and pizza sauce into a 4-cup rectangular baking tray. Stir such that the beef is coated fully in the sauce.
2. Cover with grated mozzarella and parmesan. Put your dish in the air-fryer bucket.
3. Set the temperature and adjust the clock to about 375°F for around 15 minutes.
4. When served, the dish would be brown and bubbly. Instantly serve.

3. Almond-Crusted Chicken

Preparation time: 15 minutes

Cooking time: 25 minutes

Servings: 4 people

Ingredients:

- 1 tablespoon Dijon mustard

- 2 tablespoons full-fat mayonnaise

- 2 (6-ounce) boneless, skinless chicken breasts

- 1/4 cup slivered almonds

Directions:

1. In a food processor, pulse your almonds or cut until finely diced. Put the almonds equally and put them aside on a tray.

2. Completely split each chicken breast lengthwise in part.

3. In a shallow pot, combine the mustard and mayonnaise now, cover the entire chicken with the mixture.

4. Place each piece of chicken completely coated in the diced almonds. Transfer the chicken gently into the bucket of your air fryer.

5. Set the temperature and adjust the clock to about 350°F for around 25 minutes.

6. When it has hit an interior temperature of about 165 ° F or more, the chicken will be cooked. Serve it hot.

4. Southern "Fried" Chicken

Preparation time: 15 minutes

Cooking time: 25 minutes

Servings: 4 people

Ingredients:

- 2 ounces pork rinds, finely ground
- 1/4 teaspoon ground black pepper
- 1/4 teaspoon onion powder
- 1/2 teaspoon cumin
- 1 tablespoon chili powder
- 2 tablespoons hot sauce
- 2 (6-ounce) boneless, skinless chicken breasts

Directions:

1. Longitudinally, split each chicken breast in half. Put the chicken in a big pot and add some hot sauce to coat the chicken completely.

2. Mix the onion powder, cumin, chili powder, and pepper in a shallow container. Sprinkle the mix over your chicken.

3. In a wide bowl, put the seasoned pork rinds and dunk each chicken piece into the container, covering as much as necessary. Put the chicken in the bucket of an air fryer.

4. Set the temperature and adjust the clock to about 350°F for around 25 minutes.

5. Turn the chicken gently midway through the cooking process.

6. The internal temperature will be at most 165 ° F when finished, and the coating of the pork rind will be rich golden brown in color. Serve it hot.

5. Spinach and Feta-Stuffed Chicken Breast

Preparation time: 15 minutes

Cooking time: 25 minutes

Servings: 2 people

Ingredients:

- 1 tablespoon coconut oil
- 2 (6-ounce) boneless, skinless chicken breasts
- 1/4 cup crumbled feta
- 1/4 cup chopped yellow onion
- 1/2 teaspoon salt, divided
- 1/2 teaspoon garlic powder, divided
- 5 ounces frozen spinach, thawed and drained
- 1 tablespoon unsalted butter

Directions:

1. Add some butter to your pan and sauté the spinach for around 3 minutes in a medium-sized skillet over a medium-high flame. Sprinkle the spinach with 1/4 teaspoon salt, 1/4 teaspoon garlic powder now, add your onion to the plate.

2. Sauté for another 3 minutes, then turn off the flame and put it in a medium-sized dish. Fold the feta mixture into the spinach.

3. Lengthwise, carve a nearly 4' cut through the side of each chicken breast. Scoop half of the mix into each portion and seal with a pair of toothpicks shut. Dust with leftover salt and garlic powder outside of your chicken. Drizzle some coconut oil. Put the chicken breasts in the bucket of your air fryer.

4. Set the temperature and adjust the clock to about 350°F for around 25 minutes.

5. The chicken must be golden brown in color and have an internal temperature of at least 165 ° F when fully cooked. Cut and serve hot.

6. Blackened Cajun Chicken Tenders

Preparation time: 10 minutes

Cooking time: 17 minutes

Servings: 4 people

Ingredients:

- 1/4 cup full-fat ranch dressing
- 1 pound boneless, skinless chicken tenders
- 2 tablespoons coconut oil
- 1/8 teaspoon ground cayenne pepper
- 1/4 teaspoon onion powder
- 1/2 teaspoon dried thyme
- 1/2 teaspoon garlic powder
- 1 teaspoon chili powder
- 2 teaspoons paprika

Directions:

1. Mix all the seasonings in a shallow container.
2. Drizzle oil over chicken wings and then cover each tender thoroughly in the mixture of spices. Put tenders in the bucket of your air fryer.
3. Set the temperature and adjust the clock to about 375 °F for around 17 minutes.
4. Tenders, when completely baked, will have a temperature of 165 ° F centrally.
5. For dipping, use some ranch dressing and enjoy.

7. Chicken Pizza Crust

Preparation time: 10 minutes

Cooking time: 25 minutes

Servings: 4 people

Ingredients:

1 pound ground chicken thigh meat

1/4 cup grated Parmesan cheese

1/2 cup shredded mozzarella

Directions:

1. Combine all the ingredients in a wide bowl. Split equally into four portions.

2. Slice out four (6") parchment paper circles and push down the chicken mixture on each one of the circles. Put into the bucket of your air fryer, working as required in groups or individually.

3. Set the temperature and adjust the clock to about 375°F for around 25 minutes.

4. Midway into the cooking process, turn the crust.

5. You can cover it with some cheese and your choice of toppings until completely baked, and cook for 5 extra minutes. Or, you can place the crust in the fridge or freezer and top it later when you are ready to consume.

8. Chicken Enchiladas

Preparation time: 20 minutes

Cooking time: 10 minutes

Servings: 4 people

Ingredients:

- 1 medium avocado, peeled, pitted, and sliced
- Half cup full-fat sour cream
- 1 cup shredded medium Cheddar cheese
- Half cup of torn Monterey jack (MJ) cheese
- 1/2 pound medium-sliced deli chicken
- 1/3 cup low-carb enchilada sauce, divided

- 1 1/2 cups shredded cooked chicken

Directions:

1. Combine the shredded chicken and at least half of the enchilada sauce in a big dish. On a cutting surface, lay pieces of deli chicken and pour 2 teaspoons of shredded chicken mixture on each of your slices.

2. Sprinkle each roll with 2 teaspoons of cheddar cheese. Roll softly to close it completely.

3. Put each roll, seam side down, in a 4-cup circular baking tray. Over the rolls, pour the leftover sauce and top with the Monterey Jack. Put the dish in the air-fryer basket.

4. Set the temperature and adjust the clock to about 370 °F for around 10 minutes.

5. Enchiladas, when baked, would be golden on top and bubbling. With some sour cream and diced avocado, serve hot.

9. Jalapeño Popper Hassel back Chicken

Preparation time: 20 minutes

Cooking time: 20 minutes

Servings: 4 people

Ingredients:

- 2 (6-ounce) boneless, skinless chicken breasts

- 1/4 cup sliced pickled jalapeños
- 1/2 cup shredded sharp Cheddar cheese, divided
- 2 ounces full-fat cream cheese, softened
- 4 slices sugar-free bacon, cooked and crumbled

Directions:

1. Put the fried bacon in a medium-sized dish; add in half of the cheddar, cream cheese, and the jalapeño strips.

1. Using a sharp knife to build slits around 3/4 of the way across the chicken in each of the chicken thighs, being cautious not to go all the way through. You would typically get 6 to 8 per breast, cuts based on the chicken breast's length.

2. Spoon the premade cream cheese mix onto the chicken strips. Toss the leftover shredded cheese over your chicken breasts and put it in the air fryer basket.

3. Set the temperature and adjust the clock to about 350°F for around 20 minutes.

4. Serve it hot.

10. Chicken Cordon Bleu Casserole

Preparation time: 15 minutes

Cooking time: 15 minutes

Servings: 4 people

Ingredients:

- 1-ounce pork rinds, crushed
- 2 teaspoons Dijon mustard
- 2 tablespoons unsalted butter, melted
- 1 tablespoon heavy cream

- 4 ounces full-fat cream cheese, softened
- 2 ounces Swiss cheese, cubed
- 1/2 cup cubed cooked ham
- 2 cups cubed cooked chicken thigh meat

Directions:

1. Put the chicken and ham in a 6-inch circular baking pan and toss to blend the meat uniformly. Scatter on top of the meat some cheese cubes.

2. Add butter, heavy cream, cream cheese, and mustard in a big bowl and then spill the mix over your meat and cheese. Cover with rinds of pork. Put the pan in the bucket of your air fryer.

3. Set the temperature and adjust the clock to about 350°F for around 15 minutes.

4. When finished, the saucepan will be caramelized and bubbling. Serve hot.

11.Chicken Parmesan

Preparation time: 10 minutes

Cooking time: 25 minutes

Servings: 4 people

Ingredients:

- 1-ounce pork rinds, crushed
- 1 cup low-carb, no-sugar-added pasta sauce
- 1/2 cup grated Parmesan cheese, divided
- 2 (6-ounce) boneless, skinless chicken breasts
- 1 cup shredded mozzarella cheese, divided
- 4 tablespoons full-fat mayonnaise, divided
- 1/2 teaspoon dried parsley
- 1/4 teaspoon dried oregano

- 1/2 teaspoon garlic powder

Directions:

1. Cut each chicken breast longitudinally in half and hammer it to pound out a thickness of about 3/4". Sprinkle with parsley, garlic powder, and oregano.

2. On top of each slice of chicken, scatter 1 tablespoon of mayonnaise, then cover each piece with 1/4 cup of mozzarella.

3. Mix the shredded parmesan and pork rinds in a shallow bowl. Sprinkle the surface of the mozzarella with the paste.

4. In a 6' circular baking tray, transfer the sauce and put the chicken on top. Place the pan in the bucket of your air fryer.

5. Set the temperature and adjust the clock to about 320 ° F for around 25 minutes.

6. The cheese will be light browned, and when completely baked, the chicken's internal temperature will be at about 165 ° F. Serve hot.

12. Fajita-Stuffed Chicken Breast

Preparation time: 15 minutes

Cooking time: 25 minutes

Servings: 4 people

Ingredients:

- 1/2 teaspoon garlic powder
- 1 teaspoon ground cumin
- 2 teaspoons chili powder
- 1 tablespoon coconut oil
- 1 medium green bell pepper, seeded and sliced
- 1/4 medium white onion, peeled and sliced
- 2 (6-ounce) boneless, skinless chicken breasts

Directions:

1. "Slice each chicken breast into two equal parts entirely in half longitudinally. Hammer the chicken out until it is around 1/4" thick using a meat mallet.

2. Put out each chicken slice and arrange three onion pieces and four green pepper pieces on end nearest to you. Start to firmly roll the onions and peppers into the chicken. Both with toothpicks or a few strips of butcher's twine protect the roll.

3. Drizzle the chicken with coconut oil. Sprinkle with cumin, chili powder, and garlic powder on either side. Put all the rolls in the bucket of your air fryer.

4. Set the temperature and adjust the clock to about 350°F for around 25 minutes.

5. Serve it hot.

13. Lemon Pepper Drumsticks

Preparation time: 5 minutes

Cooking time: 22 minutes

Servings: 4 people

Ingredients:

- 1 tablespoon lemon pepper seasoning
- 4 tablespoons salted butter, melted
- 8 chicken drumsticks
- 1/2 teaspoon garlic powder
- 2 teaspoons baking powder

Directions:

1. Sprinkle some baking powder over the drumsticks along with some garlic powder and massage it into the chicken skin. Add your drumsticks into the bucket of your air fryer.

2. Set the temperature and adjust the clock to about 375°F for around 25 minutes.

3. Turn your drumsticks midway through the cooking process using tongs.

4. Take out from the fryer when the skin is golden in color, and the inside temperature is at a minimum of 165 ° F.

5. Put lemon pepper seasoning and some butter in a big dish. To the dish, add your fried drumsticks and turn until the chicken is coated. Serve it hot.

14. Cilantro Lime Chicken Thighs

Preparation time: 15 minutes

Cooking time: 22 minutes

Servings: 4 people

Ingredients:

- 1/4 cup chopped fresh cilantro

- 2 medium limes

- 1 teaspoon cumin

- 2 teaspoons chili powder

- 1/2 teaspoon garlic powder

- 1 teaspoon baking powder

- 4 bone-in, skin-on chicken thighs

Directions:

1. Toss some baking powder on your chicken thighs and rinse them.

2. Mix the chili powder, garlic powder, and cumin in a small bowl and sprinkle uniformly over the thighs, rubbing softly on and under the chicken's skin.

3. Halve one lime and squeeze the liquid across the thighs. Place the chicken in the bucket of an air fryer.

4. Set the temperature and adjust the clock to about 380°F for around 22-minute.

5. For serving, split the other lime into four slices and garnish the fried chicken with lemon wedges and some cilantro.

15. Lemon Thyme Roasted Chicken

Preparation time: 10 minutes

Cooking time: 60 minutes

Servings: 6 people

Ingredients:

- 2 tablespoons salted butter, melted
- 1 medium lemon
- 1 teaspoon baking powder
- 1/2 teaspoon onion powder 2 teaspoons dried parsley
- 1 teaspoon garlic powder
- 2 teaspoons dried thyme
- 1 (4-pound) chicken

Directions:

1. Rub the garlic powder, thyme, parsley, onion powder, and baking powder with the chicken.

2. Slice the lemon put four slices using a toothpick on top of the chicken, chest side up, and secure. Put the leftover slices inside your chicken.

3. Put the whole chicken in the bucket of your air fryer, chest side down.

4. Set the temperature and adjust the clock to about 350°F for around 60-minute.

5. Switch the sides of your chicken after 30 minutes, so its breast side is up.

6. The internal temperature should be at about 165 ° F when finished, and the skin should be golden in color and crispy. Pour the melted butter over the whole chicken before serving.

16. Teriyaki Wings

Preparation time: 60 minutes

Cooking time: 45 minutes

Servings: 4 people

Ingredients:

- 2 teaspoons baking powder
- 1/4 teaspoon ground ginger
- 2 teaspoons minced garlic
- 1/2 cup sugar-free teriyaki sauce
- 2 pounds chicken wings

Directions:

1. Put all of your ingredients in a big bowl or bag, excluding the baking powder and leave to marinate in the fridge for at least 1 hour.

2. Bring the wings into the bucket of your air fryer and dust with baking powder. Rub the wings softly.

3. Set the temperature and adjust the clock to about 400°F for around 25 minutes.

4. When frying, rotate the bucket two to three times.

5. Wings, when finished, should be crunchy and cooked internally to a minimum 165 ° F. Instantly serve.

17. Crispy Buffalo Chicken Tenders

Preparation time: 15 minutes

Cooking time: 20 minutes

Servings: 4 people

Ingredients:

- 1 teaspoon garlic powder
- 1 teaspoon chili powder
- 11/2 ounces pork rinds, finely ground
- 1/4 cup hot sauce
- 1 pound boneless, skinless chicken tenders

Directions:

1. Put the chicken tenders in a big bowl and pour them over with hot sauce. In the hot sauce, toss tender, rubbing uniformly.

2. Mix the ground pork rinds with chili powder and garlic powder in a separate, wide bowl.

3. Put each tender, fully coated, in the ground pork rinds. With some water, wet your hands and push down the rinds of pork onto the chicken.

4. Put the tenders in a single layer into the basket of the air fryer.

5. Set the temperature and adjust the clock to about 375°F for around 20 minutes.

6. Serve it hot.

CHAPTER 3: Air Fryer Side Dish Recipes

1. Pita-Style Chips

Preparation time: 10 minutes

Cooking time: 5 minutes

Servings: 4 people

Ingredients:

- 1 large egg
- 1/4 cup blanched finely ground almond flour
- 1/2 ounce pork rinds, finely ground
- 1 cup shredded mozzarella cheese

Directions:

1. Put mozzarella in a wide oven-safe dish and microwave for about 30 seconds or until melted. Add the rest of the ingredients and mix until largely smooth dough shapes into a ball quickly; if your dough is too hard, microwave for an additional 15 seconds.

2. Roll the dough into a wide rectangle among two parchment paper sheets and then use a sharp knife to make the triangle-shaped chips. Put the prepared chips in the bucket of your air fryer.

3. Set the temperature and adjust the clock to about 350°F for around 5 minutes.

4. Chips, when finished, would be golden in color and crunchy. When they cool down, they will become even crispier.

2. Avocado Fries

Preparation time: 15 minutes

Cooking time: 5 minutes

Servings: 4 people

Ingredients:

- 1-ounce pork rinds, finely ground
- 2 medium avocados

Directions:

1. Split each avocado in half. Now have the pit removed. Peel the outer gently and then split the flesh into 1/4'-thick strips.

2. Put the pork rinds in a medium-sized pot and drop each slice of avocado onto your pork rinds to cover it fully. Put the pieces of avocado in the bucket of your air fryer.

3. Set the temperature and adjust the clock to about 350°F for around 5 minutes.

4. Instantly serve.

3. Flatbread

Preparation time: 5 minutes

Cooking time: 7 minutes

Servings: 2 people

Ingredients:

- 1-ounce full-fat cream cheese softened
- 1/4 cup blanched finely ground almond flour
- 1 cup shredded mozzarella cheese

Directions:

1. Meltdown some mozzarella in your microwave for about 30 seconds in a wide oven-safe container. Mix in some almond flour to make it smooth, and add some cream cheese to the mix. Proceed to blend until dough shapes, slowly kneading using wet hands if needed.

2. Split the dough into two parts and roll between two pieces of parchment paper to a thickness of about 1/4". Cut an extra piece of parchment paper to fit in the container of your air fryer.

3. Put a small piece of flatbread; try working in two batches if necessary, on your parchment paper and into the air fryer.

4. Set the temperature and adjust the clock to about 320 ° F for around 7 minutes.

5. Rotate the flatbread midway through the cooking process. Serve it hot.

4. Radish Chips

Preparation time: 10 minutes

Cooking time: 5 minutes

Servings: 4 people

Ingredients:

- 2 tablespoons coconut oil, melted
- 1/2 teaspoon garlic powder

- 1/4 teaspoon paprika
- 1/4 teaspoon onion powder
- 1 pound radishes
- 2 cups water

Directions:

1. Put the water in a medium-sized saucepan and bring the water to a boil.

2. Cut the upper part and bottom of each radish, then cut each radish thinly and evenly using a mandolin. For this stage, you can use the cutting blade in your food processor.

3. For about 5 minutes or until transparent, put the radish pieces in hot water. To trap extra humidity, extract them from the boiling water and put them on a dry paper towel.

4. In a wide pot, combine the radish pieces and the rest of the ingredients until thoroughly covered in oil and seasoned. Put the radish chips in the basket of an air fryer.

5. Set the temperature and adjust the clock to about 320°F for around 5 minutes.

6. During the cooking process, rotate the basket at least two or three times. Serve it hot.

5. Coconut Flour Cheesy Garlic Biscuits

Preparation time: 10 minutes

Cooking time: 12 minutes

Servings: 4 people

Ingredients:

- 1 scallion, sliced
- 1/2 cup shredded sharp Cheddar cheese

- 1/4 cup unsalted butter, melted and divided
- 1 large egg
- 1/2 teaspoon garlic powder
- 1/2 teaspoon baking powder
- 1/3 cup coconut flour

Directions:

1. Combine the baking powder, coconut flour, and garlic powder in a wide dish.

2. Add half the melted butter, some cheddar cheese, egg, and the scallions and mix well. Pour the mixture into a rectangular 6-inch baking tray. Put it in the basket of your air fryer.

3. Set the temperature and adjust the clock to about 320 ° F for around a 12-minute timer.

4. Take out from the pan to enable it to cool thoroughly. Slice into four parts and add leftover melted butter on top of each piece.

6. Dinner Rolls

Preparation time: 10 minutes

Cooking time: 12 minutes

Servings: 6 people

Ingredients:

- 1 large egg
- 1/2 teaspoon baking powder
- 1/4 cup ground flaxseed
- 1 cup blanched finely ground almond flour
- 1-ounce full-fat cream cheese
- 1 cup shredded mozzarella cheese

Directions:

1. In a big oven-safe dish, put the cream cheese, mozzarella, and almond flour. Microwave for about 1 minute. Blend until smooth.

2. When thoroughly mixed and soft, add baking powder, flaxseed, and egg. Suppose the dough is too hard, microwave for an extra 15 seconds.

3. Split your dough into six portions and shape it into small balls. Put the balls into the bucket of your air fryer.

4. Set the temperature and adjust the clock to about 320 ° F for around a 12-minute timer.

5. Let the rolls cool fully before serving.

7. Cilantro Lime Roasted Cauliflower

Preparation time: 10 minutes

Cooking time: 7 minutes

Servings: 4 people

Ingredients:

- 2 tablespoons chopped cilantro

- 1 medium lime
- 1/2 teaspoon garlic powder
- 2 teaspoons chili powder
- 2 tablespoons coconut oil, melted
- 2 cups chopped cauliflower florets

Directions:

1. Toss your cauliflower with coconut oil in a big dish. Dust some garlic powder and chili powder. Put the prepared cauliflower in the bucket of your air fryer.

2. Set the temperature and adjust the clock to about 350°F for around 7 minutes.

3. At the sides, the cauliflower would be soft and starting to become golden. Put in the serving dish.

4. Slice the lime and squeeze the juice over your cauliflower. Garnish using cilantro.

8. Green Bean Casserole

Preparation time: 10 minutes

Cooking time: 15 minutes

Servings: 4 people

Ingredients:

- 1/2 ounce pork rinds, finely ground
- 1 pound fresh green beans, edges trimmed
- 1/4 teaspoon xanthan gum
- 1/2 cup chicken broth
- 1-ounce full-fat cream cheese
- 1/2 cup heavy whipping cream

- 1/2 cup chopped white mushrooms
- 1/4 cup diced yellow onion
- 4 tablespoons unsalted butter

Directions:

1. Melt some butter in a medium-sized skillet over medium flame. Sauté the mushrooms and onion for around 3-5 minutes before they become tender and fragrant.

2. Transfer the cream cheese, heavy whipped cream, and broth. Mix until thick. Bring it to a boil and decrease the flame to let it simmer. Sprinkle your xanthan into the pan and turn off the flame.

3. Cut the green beans into 2-inch pieces and put them in a circular 4-cup baking tray. Pour the combination of sauce over them and swirl until they are covered. Cover the dish with the rinds of ground pork. Place it in the bucket of your air fryer.

4. Set the temperature and adjust the clock to about 320°F for around 15 minutes.

5. When completely baked, the top will be golden brown, and green beans would be fork tender. Serve it hot.

9. Buffalo Cauliflower

Preparation time: 5 minutes

Cooking time: 5 minutes

Servings: 4 people

Ingredients:

- 1/4 cup buffalo sauce
- 1/2 (1-ounce) dry ranch seasoning packet
- 2 tablespoons salted butter, melted

- 4 cups cauliflower florets

Directions:

1. Toss the cauliflower with the butter and dry the ranch in a wide pot. Place it in the bucket of your air fryer.

2. Set the temperature and adjust the clock to about 400°F for around 5 minutes.

3. During frying, rotate the basket at least two to three times. Take out the cauliflower from the fryer basket when soft, and then toss in the buffalo sauce. Serve it hot.

10. Kale Chips

Preparation time: 5 minutes

Cooking time: 5 minutes

Servings: 4 people

Ingredients:

- 1/2 teaspoon salt
- 2 teaspoons avocado oil
- 4 cups stemmed kale

Directions:

1. Toss the kale in some avocado oil in a wide bowl and dust it with some salt. Put it in the bucket of your air fryer.

2. Set the temperature and adjust the clock to about 400°F for around 5 minutes.

3. Kale, when cooked completely, would be crisp. Instantly serve.

11. Roasted Garlic

Preparation time: 5 minutes

Cooking time: 20 minutes

Servings: 12 people

Ingredients:

- 2 teaspoons avocado oil
- 1 medium head garlic

Directions:

1. Remove the garlic from any remaining excess peel. However, keep the cloves protected. Slice 1/4 of the garlic head off, showing the tops of the cloves.

2. Add your avocado oil to it. In a small layer of aluminum foil, put the garlic head, tightly enclosing it. Put it in the bucket of your air fryer.

3. Set the temperature and adjust the clock to about 400 °F for around 20 minutes. Monitor it after about 15 minutes if the garlic head is a little shorter.

4. Garlic should be nicely browned when finished and very tender.

5. Cloves can pop out to eat and be scattered or sliced quickly. Up to 2 - 5 in an airtight jar store in the fridge. You can even freeze individual cloves on a baking tray, and then put them together in a fridge-safe storage bag when frozen completely.

12. Zucchini Parmesan Chips

Preparation time: 10 minutes

Cooking time: 10 minutes

Servings: 4 people

Ingredients:

- 1/2 cup grated Parmesan cheese
- 1 large egg
- 1-ounce pork rinds
- 2 medium zucchini

Directions:

1. "Cut zucchini into thick slices of about 1/4 ". To extract excess water, put on a dry kitchen towel or two paper towels for around 30 minutes.

2. Put pork rinds and process until finely ground in the food processor. Dump into a medium-sized bowl and blend with parmesan.

3. In a shallow bowl, beat your egg.

4. Add the egg into pork rind mixture; soak zucchini pieces in it, covering as thoroughly as possible. Put each piece gently in a thin layer in the air fryer bucket, working as required in groups or individually.

5. Set the temperature and adjust the clock to about 320 degrees F for around 10 minutes.

6. Midway through the cooking process, turn your chips. Serve hot.

13. Crispy Brussels sprouts

Preparation time: 5 minutes

Cooking time: 10 minutes

Servings: 4 people

Ingredients:

- 1 tablespoon unsalted butter, melted
- 1 tablespoon coconut oil

- 1 pound Brussels sprouts

Directions:

1. Please remove all of the loose leaves from the Brussels sprouts and break them in half.

2. Sprinkle the sprouts with some coconut oil and placed them in the bowl of your air fryer.

3. Set the temperature and adjust the clock to about 400 ° F and for around10 minutes. Based on how they tend to cook, you might want to softly mix midway through the cooking period.

4. They should be soft with deeper caramelized spots when fully baked. Take out from the bucket of fryers and drizzle some melted butter. Serve instantly.

14. Cheesy Cauliflower Tots

Preparation time: 15 minutes

Cooking time: 12 minutes

Servings: 4 people

Ingredients:

- 1/8 teaspoon onion powder
- 1/4 teaspoon dried parsley
- 1/4 teaspoon garlic powder
- 1 large egg
- 1/2 cup grated Parmesan cheese
- 1 cup shredded mozzarella cheese
- 1 large head cauliflower

Directions:

1. Fill a big pot with 2 cups of water on the cooktop and put a steamer in the pot. Bring the water to a boil. Chop the cauliflower into florets and put it on a steamer bowl. Close the pot with a lid.

2. Enable cauliflower to steam for around 7 minutes before they are tender fork. Take out your cauliflower from the steamer basket and put it in a cheesecloth or dry kitchen towel, and leave it to cool down. Squeeze over the sink and extract as much extra moisture as necessary. If not all the moisture is extracted, the mixture would be too fragile to shape into tots. Crush to a smooth consistency using a fork.

3. Add in some parmesan, mozzarella, parsley, garlic powder, egg, and onion powder and place the cauliflower in a big mixing dish. Stir when thoroughly mixed. The paste should be sticky but hard to shape.

4. Roll into tot form by taking 2 teaspoons of the mix. Repeat for the remaining mixture. Put in the bucket of your air fryer.

5. Set the temperature and Adjust the clock to about 320 ° F for around 12-minute.

6. Switch tots midway through the cooking period. When fully baked, cauliflower tots should be crispy. Serve hot.

15. Sausage-Stuffed Mushroom Caps

Preparation time: 10 minutes

Cooking time: 8 minutes

Servings: 2 people

Ingredients:

- 1 teaspoon minced fresh garlic
- 1/4 cup grated Parmesan cheese
- 2 tablespoons blanched finely ground almond flour

- 1/4 cup chopped onion
- 1/2 pound Italian sausage
- 6 large Portobello mushroom caps

Directions:

1. Using a spoon, voiding scrapings, to hollow out each mushroom shell.

2. Brown the sausage for approximately 10 minutes or until thoroughly baked, and no red exists in a small-sized skillet over medium flame. Drain and then add some reserved mushroom scrapings, parmesan, almond flour, onion, and garlic. Fold ingredients softly together and proceed to cook for an extra minute, and then remove from flame.

3. Pour the mixture uniformly into mushroom caps and put the caps in a circular 6-inch pot. Put the pan in the bucket of your air fryer.

4. Set the temperature and adjust the clock to about 375 °F for around 8 minutes.

5. The tops would be browned and fizzing when it is cooked completely. Serve it hot.

16. Garlic Herb Butter Roasted Radishes

Preparation time: 10 minutes

Cooking time: 10 minutes

Servings: 4 people

Ingredients:

- black pepper
- 1/4 teaspoon ground
- 1/4 teaspoon dried oregano
- 1/2 teaspoon dried parsley
- 1/2 teaspoon garlic powder

- 2 tablespoons unsalted butter, melted
- 1 pound radishes

Directions:

1. Remove the radish roots and split them into quarters.

2. Put seasonings and butter in a shallow dish. In the herb butter, turn the radishes and put them in your air-fryer basket.

3. Set the temperature and adjust the clock to about 350°F for around 10 minutes.

4. Simply throw the radishes in the air fryer basket midway through the cooking time. Keep cooking until the edges start to turn dark brown.

5. Serve it hot.

17. Loaded Roasted Broccoli

Preparation time: 10 minutes

Cooking time: 10 minutes

Servings: 3 people

Ingredients:

- 1 scallion, sliced on the bias
- 4 slices sugar-free bacon, cooked and crumbled
- 1/4 cup full-fat sour cream
- 1/2 cup shredded sharp Cheddar cheese
- 1 tablespoon coconut oil
- 3 cups fresh broccoli florets

Directions:

1. In the air fryer basket, put the broccoli and drizzle with some coconut oil.

2. Set the temperature and adjust the clock to about 350°F for around 10 minutes.

3. During frying, turn the basket at least two to three times to prevent burning.

4. Remove from the fryer as the broccoli continues to crisp at the ends. Garnish with some scallion slices and finish with sour cream, melted cheese, and crumbled bacon.

CHAPTER 4: Air Fryer Snack and Appetizer Recipes

1. Bacon-Wrapped Brie

Preparation time: 5 minutes

Cooking time: 10 minutes

Servings: 8 people

Ingredients:

- 1 (8-ounce) round Brie
- 4 slices sugar-free bacon

Directions:

1. To shape an X, position two bacon strips. Put the third bacon strip over the middle of the X sideways. Position vertically over the X a fourth slice of bacon. On top of your X, it could appear like an addition sign (+). Position the Brie in the middle of the bacon.

2. Tie the bacon from around Brie, using several toothpicks to hold it. To suit your air-fryer container, take a piece of parchment paper and put your bacon-wrapped Brie on it. Put it in the container of your air fryer.

3. Set the temperature and set the clock to about 400°F for around 10 minutes.

4. When there are only 3 minutes left on the clock, rotate Brie gently.

5. The bacon will be crispy when grilled, and the cheese will be smooth and melted. Cut into eight pieces to serve.

2. Crust less Meat Pizza

Preparation time: 5 minutes

Cooking time: 5 minutes

Servings: 1 people

Ingredients:

- 2 tablespoons low-carb, sugar-free pizza sauce for dipping
- 1 tablespoon grated or cutup Parmesan cheese
- 2 slices sugar-free bacon, cooked and crumbled
- 1/4 cup cooked ground sausage
- 7 slices pepperoni
- 1/2 cup shredded mozzarella cheese

Directions:

1. Line the bottom of a mozzarella 6' cake tray. Put on top of your cheese some sausage, pepperoni, and bacon and cover with parmesan. Put the pan in the bowl of your air fryer.

2. Set the temperature and set the clock to about 400°F for around 5 minutes.

3. Remove from the flame once the cheese is fizzing and lightly golden. Serve hot with some pizza sauce as dipping.

3. Garlic Cheese Bread

Preparation time: 10 minutes

Cooking time: 10 minutes

Servings: 2 people

Ingredients:

- 1/2 teaspoon garlic powder
- 1 large egg1 large egg
- 1/4 cup grated Parmesan cheese
- 1 cup shredded mozzarella cheese1 cup shredded mozzarella cheese

Directions:

1. In a big bowl, combine all the ingredients. To fit your air fryer bowl cut a piece of parchment paper. Add the blend onto the parchment paper to form a circle and put it in the air fryer basket.

2. Set the temperature and adjust the timer to about 350°F for around 10 minutes.

3. Serve it hot.

4. Mozzarella Pizza Crust

Preparation time: 5 minutes

Cooking time: 10 minutes

Servings: 1 people

Ingredients:

- 1 large egg white
- 1 tablespoon full-fat cream cheese
- 2 tablespoons blanched finely ground almond flour
- 1/2 cup shredded whole-milk mozzarella cheese

Directions:

1. In a small oven-safe bowl, put almond flour, mozzarella, and cream cheese. Microwave for about 30 seconds. Mix until the mixture becomes a softball. Add egg white and mix until fluffy, circular dough forms.

2. Shape into 6 round crust pizza.

3. To suit your air fryer container, take a piece of parchment paper and put each crust on the parchment paper. Place it in the basket of your air fryer.

4. Set the temperature and adjust the clock to about 350°F for around 10 minutes.

5. Switch sides after 5 minutes and put any preferred toppings on your crust at this stage. Keep cooking until lightly golden. Immediately serve.

5. Spicy Spinach Artichoke Dip

Preparation time: 10 minutes

Cooking time: 10 minutes

Servings: 6 people

Ingredients:

- 1 cup shredded pepper jack cheese
- 1/4 cup grated Parmesan cheese
- 1/2 teaspoon garlic powder
- 1/4 cup full-fat sour cream
- 1/4 cup full-fat mayonnaise
- 8 ounces full-fat cream cheese, softened
- 1/4 cup chopped pickled jalapeños
- 1 (14-ounce) can artichoke hearts, drained and chopped
- 10 ounces frozen spinach, drained and thawed

Directions:

1. In a 4-cup baking dish, combine all your ingredients. Put it in the basket of your air fryer.

2. Set the temperature and adjust the timer for around 10 minutes to about 320 °F.

3. When dark brown and sizzling, remove from flame. Serve it hot.

6. Mini Sweet Pepper Poppers

Preparation time: 18 minutes

Cooking time: 8 minutes

Servings: 4 people

Ingredients:

- 1/4 cup shredded pepper jack cheese
- 4 slices sugar-free bacon, cooked and crumbled
- 4 ounces full-fat cream cheese, softened
- 8 mini sweet peppers

Directions:

1. Cut the tops of your peppers and lengthwise cut each one in the quarter. Remove the seeds and cut the membranes with a tiny knife.

2. Toss the bacon, cream cheese, and pepper jack in a tiny bowl.

3. Put each sweet pepper with 3 tsp. of the mixture and push down smoothly. Put it in the air fryer basket.

4. Set the temperature and adjust the clock to about 400°F for around 8 minutes.

5. Serve it hot.

7. Bacon-Wrapped Onion Rings

Preparation time: 5 minutes

Cooking time: 10 minutes

Servings: 4 people

Ingredients:

- 8 slices sugar-free bacon
- 1 tablespoon sriracha
- 1 large onion, peeled

Directions:

1. Cut your onion into large 1/4-inch pieces. Sprinkle the sriracha on the pieces of your onion. Take two pieces of onion and cover the circles with bacon. Redo with the rest of the onion and bacon. Put in the container of your air fryer.

2. Set the temperature and adjust the clock to about 350°F for around 10 minutes.

3. To rotate the onion rings midway through the frying period, use tongs. The bacon would be crispy once completely fried. Serve hot.

8. Mozzarella Sticks

Preparation time: 60 minutes

Cooking time: 10 minutes

Servings: 4 people

Ingredients:

- 2 big eggs
- 1 teaspoon dried parsley
- 1/2 ounce pork rinds, finely ground
- 1/2 cup of grated Parmesan or any other kind of cheese
- 6 (1-ounce) mozzarella string cheese sticks

Directions:

1. Put mozzarella sticks on a chopping board and slice in half. Freeze for about 45 minutes or till solid. Remove your frozen sticks after an hour if freezing overnight, then put them in a sealed zip-top plastic bag and put them back for potential usage in the freezer.
2. Mix the ground pork rinds, parmesan, and parsley in a wide dish.
3. Whisk the eggs together in a medium dish separately.
4. Soak a stick of frozen mozzarella into whisked eggs and then cover in Parmesan mixture. Repeat for the leftover sticks. Put the sticks of mozzarella in the basket of your air fryer.
5. Set the temperature to about 400 degrees F and adjust the clock for around 10 minutes or till it turns golden.
6. Serve it hot.

9. Pork Rind Tortillas

Preparation time: 10 minutes

Cooking time: 5 minutes

Servings: 4 people

Ingredients:

- 1 large egg

- 2 tablespoons full-fat cream cheese
- 3/4 cup shredded mozzarella cheese
- 1-ounce pork rinds

Directions:

1. Put pork rinds and pulses into the food processor pulse till finely ground.

2. Put mozzarella in a big oven-safe bowl. Cut the cream cheese into tiny bits and transfer them to the bowl. Microwave for about 30 seconds or so; all cheeses are molten and can be combined into a ball quickly. To the cheese mixture, add some ground pork rinds and eggs.

3. Keep mixing until the combination forms a ball. If it cools too fast and the cheese hardens, microwave for another 10 seconds.

4. Divide the dough into four tiny balls. Put each dough ball among 2 pieces of parchment paper and roll into a 1/4" flat layer.

5. Put the tortilla chips in a thin layer in your air fryer basket, operating in groups if required.

6. Set the temperature and adjust the clock to about 400°F for around 5 minutes.

7. Tortillas, when thoroughly baked, would be crispy and solid.

8. Instantly serve.

10. Bacon Cheeseburger Dip

Preparation time: 20 minutes

Cooking time: 10 minutes

Servings: 6 people

Ingredients:

- 2 large pickle spears, chopped
- 6 slices sugar-free bacon, cooked and crumbled

- 1/2 pound cooked 80/20 ground beef
- 11/4 cups shredded medium Cheddar cheese, divided
- 1 tablespoon Worcestershire sauce
- 1 teaspoon garlic powder
- 1/4 cup chopped onion
- 1/4 cup full-fat sour cream
- 1/4 cup full-fat mayonnaise
- 8 ounces full-fat cream cheese

Directions:

1. Put the cream cheese in a big, oven-safe dish and microwave for about 45 seconds. Add the Worcestershire sauce, sour cream, mayonnaise, garlic powder, onion, and 1 cup of Cheddar and mix well. Add fried ground beef and your bacon to it. Sprinkle the leftover Cheddar on top of the mixture.

2. Put in a 6-inch bowl and dump into the basket of your air fryer.

3. Set the temperature and adjust the clock to about 400°F for around 10 minutes.

4. When the surface is golden brown and bubbling, dipping is cooked. Scatter pickles over the dish. Serve hot.

11. Pizza Rolls

Preparation time: 18 minutes

Cooking time: 10 minutes

Servings: 8 people

Ingredients:

- 2 tablespoons grated Parmesan cheese
- 1/2 teaspoon dried parsley
- 1/4 teaspoon garlic powder
- 2 tablespoons unsalted butter, melted
- 8 (1-ounce) mozzarella string cheese sticks, cut into 3 pieces each
- 72 slices pepperoni
- 2 large eggs
- 1/2 cup almond flour
- 2 cups shredded mozzarella cheese

Directions:

1. Put almond flour and mozzarella in a big oven-safe bowl. Microwave for a minute. Withdraw the bowl and blend until a ball of dough forms. If required, microwave for an extra 30 seconds.

2. Crack the eggs into your bowl and blend until the ball becomes soft dough. Wet your hands with some water and gently knead your dough.

3. Rip off two wide pieces of parchment paper and brush with nonstick cooking spray on each side. Put your dough ball between the 2 pieces, facing dough with coated sides. To roll dough to a thickness of 1/4', use a rolling pin.

4. To cut into 24 rectangles, use a cutter. Put three pepperoni pieces and 1 strip of stringed cheese on each one of your rectangle.

5. Fold the rectangle in two, lining the filling with cheese and pepperoni. Ends closed by squeeze or roll. To suit your air-fryer bowl, take a piece of parchment paper and put it in the basket. On the parchment paper, place the rolls.

6. Set the temperature and adjust the clock to about 350°F for around 10 minutes.

7. Open your fryer after 5 minutes and rotate the rolls of pizza. Resume the fryer and proceed to cook until the rolls of pizza are golden brown.

8. Put the garlic powder, butter, and parsley in a tiny bowl. Brush the mix over the rolls of fried pizza and scatter the pizza with parmesan. Serve it hot.

12. Bacon Jalapeño Cheese Bread

Preparation time: 10 minutes

Cooking time: 18 minutes

Servings: 4 people

Ingredients:

- 4 slices sugar-free bacon, cooked and chopped
- 2 large eggs
- 1/4 cup chopped pickled jalapeños
- 1/4 cup of grated Parmesan cheese
- 2 cups shredded mozzarella cheese

Directions:

1. In a wide bowl, combine all your ingredients. Cut a slice of parchment to match the basket of your air fryer.

2. With a touch of water, dampen both of your hands and spread the mix out into a disk. Depending on the fryer's scale, you would need to split this into 2 small cheese bread.

3. Put the parchment paper and your cheese bread into the basket of the air fryer.

4. Set the temperature and adjust the clock to about 320°F for around 15 minutes.

5. Turn the bread gently once you have 5 minutes remaining.

6. The top would be golden brown when completely baked. Serve it hot.

13. Spicy Buffalo Chicken Dip

Preparation time: 10 minutes

Cooking time: 10 minutes

Servings: 4 people

Ingredients:

- 2 scallions, sliced on the bias
- 11/2 cups shredded medium Cheddar cheese, divided
- 1/3 cup chopped pickled jalapeños
- 1/3 cup full-fat ranch dressing

- 1/2 cup buffalo sauce
- 8 ounces full-fat cream cheese, softened
- 1 cup cooked, diced chicken breast

Directions:

1. Put the chicken in a spacious bowl. Add some ranch dressing, cream cheese, and buffalo sauce. Mix until the sauces are fully blended and completely soft. Fold the jalapeños along with 1 cup of Cheddar in it.

2. Transfer the mixture into a circular 4-cup baking dish and put the leftover Cheddar on top. Put the dish in your air-fryer basket.

3. Set the temperature and adjust the clock to about 350°F for around 10 minutes.

4. When cooked, it'll be brown at the top, and the dip will bubble. Serve it hot with some cut-up scallions on top.

14. Garlic Parmesan Chicken Wings

Preparation time: 4 minutes

Cooking time: 25 minutes

Servings: 4 people

Ingredients:

- 1/4 teaspoon dried parsley
- 1/3 cup grated Parmesan cheese
- 4 tablespoons unsalted butter, melted
- 1 tablespoon baking powder
- 1/2 teaspoon garlic powder
- 1 teaspoon pink Himalayan salt
- 2 pounds raw chicken wings

Directions:

1. Put the chicken wings, 1/2 teaspoon of garlic powder, salt, and baking powder in a wide bowl, then toss. Put the wings in the basket of your air fryer.

2. Set the temperature and adjust the clock to about 400°F for around 25 minutes.

3. During the cooking period, rotate the bowl two to three times to ensure even cooking.

4. Mix the parmesan, butter, and parsley in a shallow dish.

5. Please take out your wings from the fryer and put them in a big, clean dish. Over your wings, pour the butter mixture and toss until covered completely. Serve it hot.

15. Bacon-Wrapped Jalapeño Poppers

Preparation time: 16 minutes

Cooking time: 12 minutes

Servings: 5 people

Ingredients:

- 12 slices sugar-free bacon
- 1/4 teaspoon garlic powder
- 1/3 cup shredded medium Cheddar cheese
- 3 ounces full-fat cream cheese
- 6 jalapeños (about 4" long each)

Directions:

1. Slice off the tops of the jalapeños and cut lengthwise down the middle into two sections. Using a knife to gently detach the white membrane and seeds from the peppers.

2. Put the Cheddar, cream cheese, and garlic powder in a big, oven-proof dish. Stir in the microwave for about 30 seconds. Spoon the blend of cheese into your hollow jalapeño.

3. Place a bacon slice over each half of the jalapeño, totally covering the pepper. Place it in the basket of an air fryer.

4. Set the temperature and adjust the clock to about 400°F for around 12 minutes.

5. Flip the peppers halfway into the cooking period. Serve it hot.

16. Prosciutto-Wrapped Parmesan Asparagus

Preparation time: 10 minutes

Cooking time: 10 minutes

Servings: 4 people

Ingredients:

- 2 tablespoons salted butter, melted
- 1/3 cup grated Parmesan cheese
- 1/8 teaspoon red pepper flakes
- 2 teaspoons lemon juice
- 1 tablespoon coconut oil, melted

- 12 (0.5-ounce) slices prosciutto
- 1 pound asparagus

Directions:

1. Put an asparagus spear on top of a slice of prosciutto on a clean cutting board.

2. Drizzle with coconut oil and lemon juice. Sprinkle the asparagus with parmesan and red pepper flakes. Roll prosciutto across a spear of asparagus. Put it in the basket of your air fryer.

3. Set the temperature and adjust the clock to about 375 °F for around 10 minutes or so.

4. Dribble the asparagus roll with some butter before serving.

CHAPTER 5: Desserts

1. Mini Cheesecake

Preparation time: 10 minutes

Cooking time: 15-18 minutes

Servings: 2 people

Ingredients:

- 1/8 cup powdered erythritol
- 1/2 teaspoon vanilla extract
- 1 large egg
- 4 ounces full-fat cream cheese, softened
- 2 tablespoons granular erythritol
- 2 tablespoons salted butter
- 1/2 cup walnuts

Directions:

1. In a food mixer, put the butter, walnuts, and granular erythritol. Pulse until the items bind together to shape the dough.
2. Push the dough into a 4-inch spring form pan and put the pan in the bucket of your air fryer.
3. Set the temperature and adjust the clock to about 400°F for around 5 minutes.
4. Pick the crust when the timer dings, and let it cool.
5. Mix your cream cheese with the vanilla extract, egg, and powdered erythritol in a medium-sized bowl until creamy.

2. Pecan Brownies

Preparation time: 10 minutes

Cooking time: 20 minutes

Servings: 6 people

Ingredients:

- 1/4 cup low-carb, sugar-free chocolate chips
- 1/4 cup chopped pecans
- 1 large egg
- 1/4 cup unsalted butter, softened
- 1/2 teaspoon baking powder
- 2 tablespoons unsweetened cocoa powder
- 1/2 cup powdered erythritol
- 1/2 cup blanched finely ground almond flour

Directions:

1. Mix the almond flour, chocolate powder, erythritol, and baking powder in a big bowl. Stir in the egg and butter.

2. "Fold in the chocolate chips and pecans. Pour the mixture into a 6" circular baking tray. Place the pan in the bucket of your air fryer.

3. Set the temperature and adjust the clock to about 300°F for around 20 minutes.

4. A toothpick placed in the middle will fall out clean once completely fried. Please enable it to cool off entirely and firm up for about 20 minutes.

3. Cinnamon Sugar Pork Rinds

Preparation time: 5 minutes

Cooking time: 5 minutes

Servings: 2 people

Ingredients:

- 1/4 cup powdered erythritol
- 1/2 teaspoon ground cinnamon

- 2 tablespoons unsalted butter, melted
- 2 ounces pork rinds

Directions:

1. Toss the pork rinds and butter into a wide pan. Sprinkle some erythritol and cinnamon, and toss to cover uniformly.

2. Put the pork rinds into the bucket of your air fryer.

3. Set the temperature and adjust the clock to about 400°F for around 5 minutes.

4. Instantly serve.

4. Almond Butter Cookie Balls

Preparation time: 5 minutes

Cooking time: 10 minutes

Servings: 10 people

Ingredients:

- 1/2 teaspoon ground cinnamon
- 1/4 cup low-carb, sugar-free chocolate chips
- 1/4 cup shredded unsweetened coconut
- 1/4 cup powdered erythritol
- 1/4 cup low-carb protein powder
- 1 teaspoon vanilla extract
- 1 large egg
- 1 cup almond butter

Directions:

1. Mix the almond butter with the egg in a big pot. Add protein powder, vanilla, and erythritol to it.

2. Fold in the coconut, chocolate chips, and cinnamon. Roll into 1" spheres. Put the balls in a 6' circular baking tray and place them in the bucket of your air fryer.

3. Set the temperature and adjust the clock to about 10 minutes to around 320 °F.

4. Please enable it to cool fully. Up to 4 days in an airtight jar placed in the fridge.

Conclusion

These times, air frying is one of the most common cooking techniques and air fryers have become one of the chef's most impressive devices. In no time, air fryers can help you prepare nutritious and tasty meals! To prepare unique dishes for you and your family members, you do not need to be a master in the kitchen!

Everything you have to do is buy an air fryer and this wonderful cookbook for air fryers! Soon, you can make the greatest dishes ever and inspire those around you.

Cooked meals at home with you! Believe us! Get your hands on an air fryer and this handy set of recipes for air fryers and begin your new cooking experience! Have fun!

The 15-Day Men's Health Book of 15-Minute Workouts

The Time-Saving Program to Raise a Leaner, Stronger, More Muscular You

Giovanni Paletto

Table of Contents

Introduction

The 15-minute workout is a revolutionary idea. Most of us have been taught that a good workout takes 45 to 60 minutes, three or four times a week. But the benefits we get from the time spent exercising last only as long as we can push ourselves—and sometimes even less than that. Even those who exercise six days a week for 50 minutes each time rarely lose weight, build muscle or gain strength to any significant degree because their bodies adapt quickly to the demands they are placing on them. That's why I've developed this 15-minute program so you can get stronger, leaner and healthier without having to spend hours at the gym. You'll get leaner, stronger and better at burning off body fat—and you'll do it in less time than it takes to watch an hour-long TV series.

The 15-minute workout is based on simple exercise science. Researchers have known for decades that our bodies adapt quickly to the demands we place on them through exercise. When that happens, we stop getting as much benefit from the workouts we're doing. It's a concept called overtraining or spiking cortisol levels: The stress of regular workouts increases your cortisol levels, which makes you tired when you should be energized. Over time, you will stop seeing progress because your muscles will begin to stop responding to the training. The only way to overcome this adaptation is to keep increasing the intensity of your workouts—and that can spell trouble for your body.

Even high-intensity interval training—the kind of workout where people alternate periods of strenuous exercise with periods of rest—will only give you a couple of weeks of results before your body adapts. You'll get stronger, but you'll also get leaner and faster, and then…nothing.

Why? Because one way our bodies store energy is by enhancing its sensitivity to insulin, which helps it use fat as fuel. This adaptation is good for endurance activities like running or biking, since it helps your body get energy from stored fat. But it's not so good if you want to lose weight and burn body fat. The only way to overcome this adaptation is to keep increasing the intensity of your workouts—and that can spell trouble for your body.

The 15-minute workout works differently from traditional training because it takes advantage of what exercise scientists call the "pump effect" and "metabolic chaos": short bursts of intense activity followed by brief spurts of rest—all performed in 15 minutes or less. During and immediately after a workout, your body is flooded with stress hormones that boost your metabolism and increase fat burning. The 15-minute workout also keeps cortisol levels from spiking, which means you'll feel energized for hours after you exercise.

The 15-minute workout will give you a leaner, stronger body and a calmer mind—but it's important to realize that it won't give the same benefits as those long workouts you're used to. You won't see the same results in terms of strength and endurance because your body won't have enough time to adapt to the increased intensity. The good news is that most of this adaptation occurs in the first 15 minutes of your workout, and after that, you can just focus on having fun, getting healthier and feeling better.

The magic combination for the 15-minute workout is a mix of intense weight training and fast intervals of cardio. I have designed two different programs based on these principles—one for total-body leanness (which includes a full-body circuit) and one for building strength. Both use simple exercises you can do with a barbell for weight training, a pair of dumbbells at home or nothing more than your own body weight.

Chapter 1: The Science of 15-Minute Workouts

The best exercise, the most effective way to lose weight and get lean and healthy, takes place in the first 15 minutes of your workout. By "best" I mean that this type of workout is more effective than longer workouts because it boosts your body's metabolism and helps you burn fat. And by "least effective," I mean that workouts over an hour turn out to be counterproductive for most people, especially those who want to lose weight and build muscle. To be clear, this doesn't mean any exercise is better than no exercise. It just means that the kind of workout that offers the best results in the shortest period of time takes place in the first 15 minutes of your training sessions.

Advantages Over Traditional Workouts

1. It increases your metabolism and burns fat for hours after you exercise.

2. It keeps cortisol levels from spiking, which means you'll feel energized for hours after you exercise.

3. It's more effective in terms of building cardiovascular fitness than longer, less intense workouts (though if you get out of breath or lightheaded during your workouts, take a break and have a glass of water).

4. It leads to better weight loss than longer, less intense workouts because it helps you burn more fat in the hours following your workout (this point is debatable; see Chapter 7).

5. Your muscles respond positively to this type of workout with visible results; your body begins to shape up within two weeks.

6. It is more effective than longer, less intense workouts in terms of increasing muscle strength and endurance.

7. It keeps you focused on the workout itself, so you don't waste time worrying about what you're wearing or how much time the guy next to you lifts weights.

8. It's perfect for busy people who can't commit to longer exercise sessions (but even those who can devote an hour or more to their workout will benefit from including shorter sessions in their week).

9. It improves your mood and mental health because it boosts endorphins and helps reduce stress levels — even during a stressful day at the office.

Disadvantages Over Traditional Workouts
1. It is tough for beginners.

2. It takes up more time in your day than longer, less intense workouts do (though you can incorporate it into your busy life without much fuss).

3. It's not easy to stay motivated; you can feel like you're not doing enough in the beginning when your body is still adjusting to this type of training.

4. Some experts say shorter workouts aren't an effective way to build muscle, but the research I've cited tells a different story.

5. It can be very hard on your joints and spine.

6. It places a lot of stress on your body, which may lead to injury.

7. You're going to feel sore the next day (which is why this type of workout works best if you plan it for before work or on weekends).

8. You risk overtraining—doing too much too soon—which could leave you vulnerable to injury and burnout.

9. It might actually make weight loss harder because some studies show that working out intensely boosts your appetite.

10. Some people get bored doing shorter workouts, but you can switch up your routine to help stop this from happening.

11. You're more susceptible to skipping a workout or falling off the fitness wagon.

12. You may lack the energy to perform other activities in your day-to-day life, which is not what you want if you're trying to be healthy!

13. Some short workouts don't offer all of the health benefits that they claim (or any at all).

The most effective way to make sure you're benefiting from your workout regimen is to do workouts that are 30 minutes or longer. This is why an hour-long session at a gym, yoga studio, or fitness class works best - it takes about fifty minutes for your brain and body to be engaged enough to use the movements effectively while you're building endurance and strength. If you notice yourself struggling the first time you try something new, stick with it and don't give up until you can reap all of the benefits of the workout. And if you find yourself struggling with motivation, try pairing up with a friend! You can motivate each other; plus, research shows we work out more frequently when we have a buddy.

The length of your workout matters because it determines what is happening in your brain and body. Shorter workouts, even if they are intense, won't give you the same benefits as longer workouts. Even if you feel like you're getting leaner and stronger with your short workout, it could be that the change is not due to the workout improving your muscle tone or endurance - it might just be that your body is getting better at burning off fat and conserving energy.

You might think that some forms of exercise are more effective than others, but the duration of a workout is not what you should be focusing on. What really matters is that you participate in a workout that gets your heart rate up, improves your endurance and works your muscles. The type of training most people use to "get in shape" at gyms these days falls into two camps: interval training and resistance training. The problem with these two types of training is that they can be very hard on your body if performed too frequently over too long a duration. The interval training that fitness junkies are so fond of doesn't work for everyone—especially if you're new to the activity or have a bad hip. Resistance training is all about strength-building, which is why I designed the resistance program at FitnessBlueprint.com. It's one thing to get stronger, but why focus on it when endurance and fat-burning are your real goals? That's why I created a workout that focuses on fat burning and building muscular endurance without putting your body through hard intervals of cardio or stressful resistance training. To do it, you'll have to keep your heart rate up and your muscles working, but you don't have to put your body through tough intervals over and over again. The rest of this book will explain the science behind this exercise program — and how it can help you get leaner, stronger and fitter in just 15 minutes a day.

Chapter 2: Maximizing Your Weight-Training Workouts

The best weight-training sessions last about 45 to 60 minutes, and they're designed to help you build lean muscle mass. Of course, that's not what we're going for. Our goal is to lose fat and improve our health, which is why I have designed a set of 15-minute workouts that will increase your metabolism and burn fat after each workout. These workouts are less intense than those traditional weight-training sessions that last an hour or more, and they don't require the same amount of time from you. You don't need to go to the gym and spend hours on exercise machines. You can lift weights using your own body weight, or you can use barbells and dumbbells you have at home. The workouts are simple, but that doesn't mean they're easy. To make them effective, you'll need to push yourself—and work through that discomfort you might feel if this is your first time doing a workout like this or if it has been a long time since you have done a good weight-training session. I designed this program to help build muscle mass using basic barbell exercises that work every muscle in your body - including your chest, back, shoulders, abs and legs. Your muscles will be responding to this type of training within two weeks, and you can expect that they will change in terms of appearance and performance. Not everyone wants to look like a bodybuilder, but most people want to look better. And this program—which takes place over just seven days—will help you do just that. You'll gain more muscle and lose more fat than you would with an hour-long, traditional workout. And even though this program is focused on building muscle, it will help you burn calories through the work your muscles do. It doesn't matter if you want to lose five pounds or 50 — every workout you do shapes your body in some way. This program is for everyone because it uses compound exercises that work multiple muscles at once. If you are very out of shape, the 15-minute workouts will help you burn calories, improve your endurance and lift more than you ever have before. If you are already in good shape but want to get even stronger or more toned, this program will help. If your goal is to just build muscle and stay healthy, this is the program for you. Every workout will help you get stronger, which is what building muscle mass is all about. And you can expect to start noticing visible results within the first two weeks. Your muscles will be much firmer, your biceps will be more defined, your abs will be more pronounced and your legs will look leaner. If you already have some muscle mass or you spend the time to really work out those areas that need it, you can expect to see a difference in how your body looks in about six weeks. There is no such thing as spot reduction - where one area of your body (your butt, for example) gets smaller while another part (like your thighs) gets bigger - but this program does help promote lean muscle mass throughout the entire body. Every workout session burns calories and elevates the metabolism for hours after you've finished exercising. You'll also notice that your clothes fit better because you're leaner, and there will be fat burning 24/7.

This workout will help you create a calorie deficit - the difference between the calories you eat and the calories you burn off. The more time passes, the bigger that calorie deficit gets, which means you lose more weight faster. If your goal is to lose about 1 to 2 pounds per week, this workout will help you get there. Whether this is your first weight-training program or not, each session should feel just as intense as it does for someone who is just starting out at the gym. If you aren't feeling the burn or you are feeling fatigued, you are not pushing yourself hard enough. Push through your workouts. Every time you work out, you should be able to do more of the exercises than the last time.

Repeat each set of exercises twice. You can do each set back-to-back or rest 1 to 3 minutes in between before moving on to your next set. Rest 1 to 3 minutes between each round, and complete four rounds in total. Rest 1 day before moving on to the next workout session.

1. Chest Press

This exercise targets your pectoralis major, and it's a great way to build your chest if you are new to weight training or have been away from the gym for awhile. To do it, place a barbell on your upper back. You can use an Olympic bar or an EZ curl bar. Step underneath the bar and squat down low while holding onto its ends. Stand up straight while holding the bar with both hands at shoulder width.

2. Rear Deltoid Flyes

This is another great exercise for beginners because it doesn't require much knowledge about form or equipment. All you need is a bench and some dumbbells. Sit on the edge of the bench with your back facing the ceiling. Grab one dumbbell and rest it on your chest. Lower it out to the side while keeping your arms straight and elbows close to your body. Slowly bring it back up, squeeze your chest muscles and repeat for 10 reps on each side.

3. Triceps Dips

This exercise targets the triceps, which are some of the largest muscles in your upper arms. To do them, place a chair or bench so that it is standing behind you high enough that you can comfortably bend over and rest your weight on it without falling off. Place your hands on the edge of the bench with your fingers pointing towards you. Bend your legs under you and lower yourself until you feel a light stretch in your triceps. Press yourself back up, straighten your arms and repeat for 10 reps.

4. Dumbbell Curls

This exercise will help strengthen your biceps, which are the muscles in the front of your upper arms. Grab a set of light dumbbells - even a 2-pound set will work if that's all you have on hand at home - and stand with your feet shoulder-width apart. Keep your arms straight with a slight bend at the elbow, and lift them up towards your shoulders without moving them forward or back as you curl them up towards you chest. Squeeze your biceps at the top of the movement, and slowly bring them back to the starting position. Repeat for 8 to 10 reps.

5. Reverse Crunch

This exercise will help strengthen your core muscles, which are the ones in your abdomen and lower back. Lie on the floor with your knees bent up near your chest and feet flat on the ground. Place both hands behind your head or underneath your neck with elbows out (like you were going for an upside down push up). Lift yourself off of the ground by tightening in abs and pulling yourself up as if you were trying to touch your feet with your chest. Squeeze your abdominals as you exhale, and slowly lower yourself back down to the floor. Repeat for 10 reps.

6. One-Legged Dead Lift

This exercise will help strengthen your hamstrings and glutes, which are some of the largest muscles in the back of your legs. To do it, grab a barbell with a wide grip near the ends of its handle (but not so wide that it is hard to hold). Stand up straight with your feet shoulder-width apart and knees facing forward so that the barbell is hanging in front of you. Slowly bend at the waist while keeping your back straight and pulling down on the barbell with both hands until you feel a stretch in your hamstrings.

Chapter 3: Cardio and Mind-Body Training

The best cardio workouts last about 45 to 60 minutes—and they can lead to a leaner body. That's how long it takes to get your heart rate up, burn calories and elevate the metabolism. That's also not what we're going for. Our goal here is to burn fat, which is why I have designed a set of 15-minute workouts that will help you access your fat stores and burn more fat after each workout. These workouts don't require the same amount of time from you because they aren't as intense as traditional cardio sessions that last an hour or more. But don't let that fool you— this isn't a light workout by any means. You will definitely feel them the next day because it takes a lot of work to burn calories and to build endurance. But the good thing is, you'll look forward to your workouts when they're over and you realize how much of a difference they are making in your life. This program will help you burn calories soon after each workout thanks to that calorie-burning effect called excess post-exercise oxygen consumption, or EPOC. You can think of EPOC as the afterburn effect, which makes it so that even after you are finished exercising, your body continues working for up to 24 hours after every workout session and burns more fat during that time. The only way to get this effect is to burn a lot of fat. The workouts in this program will help you do that. There are seven workout sessions in the program, and each one will last 15 minutes. I designed those short workouts to maximize your time and your results. They will help you burn calories and build endurance without being too intense or taking up too much time from your day. Each workout session uses a different cardio exercise so that you don't get bored from doing the same thing every day. Your muscles, joints and ligaments need rest in between exercises - especially if you are new to barbell training or resistance training in general. This program assumes that you are starting out with a basic understanding of how to lift weights, or that you have already gained enough control over your body and its movements to be able to complete the exercises safely. If you aren't sure if this program is right for you, talk with a certified trainer or fitness professional who can help you decide whether or not it is a good fit for your current fitness level.

To get the most out of this workout plan, do each session 2 or 3 times per week. You can do it every other day, but I would recommend spacing them out by at least two days so that your muscles have some time to repair themselves between training sessions. If you are just starting out, you might want to choose a lighter exercise session for days when you are doing your upper body workout. If you aren't sure which workout session is right for your fitness level, talk with a certified trainer or fitness professional who can help you decide.

1. Bodyweight Squats

This is a great way to warm up before your workout. It's not only good for building strength and increasing flexibility, it also burns calories. Stand with your feet shoulder-width apart and hold your arms out in front of you at shoulder height with palms facing down. Lean your weight back into your heels, and lower yourself towards the ground while flexing your knees to 90 degrees. Keep going until you feel a light stretch in your calves or thighs, then press back up and repeat for 50 reps.

2. Pushups

This is another great workout to do as a warm-up. Pushups are a compound exercise that work out your chest, abs and shoulders, and they also help strengthen your triceps and biceps. To do them, lie facedown with your hands spread out about shoulder-width apart underneath you. Lower yourself towards the ground until your chest nearly touches it while keeping your elbows at 90 degrees. Press yourself back up to the starting position by pushing with your arms, shoulders and chest. Repeat for 50 reps.

3. Lunge Jumps With Pushup

This is a bodyweight exercise that will definitely get you sweating! To do it, start in a standing position with feet shoulder-width apart and hands on hips. Step forward with one foot about two and a half feet out from your body, and bend both knees until you feel a light stretch in your thigh. Your back knee should be nearly touching the ground, but keep it just an inch off the ground without letting it touch. Press yourself back up to the starting position by pushing with your front leg muscles, then jump up as high as you can and land softly on the ground in the same position you were in when you started. Repeat for 15 reps on each leg.

4. Skaters

This is another compound exercise that will get your heart pumping! To do this exercise, stand with feet shoulder-width apart and arms out at your sides with palms facing forward. Jump up and down on your toes, and move your arms back and forth in a running motion while you jump. The faster you are moving your arms, the easier it will be to get your heart rate up. Repeat for 25 jumps.

5. Leg Lifts

This exercise is great for toning and strengthening your lower abdominal area! Start lying on the floor with legs together and arms at your sides with palms facing down. Raise both legs off the ground as high as you can by bringing in both the front and back sides of both legs. Squeeze those same muscles on the way back down to the starting position, then repeat for 15 reps.

6. Walking Lunges

This bodyweight exercise is one of my favourites - it exercises so many different muscles at once! Stand with your feet shoulder-width apart and arms out in front of you at shoulder height with palms facing down. Step forward with one foot about two and a half feet out from your body, and bend both knees until you feel a light stretch in your thigh. Your back knee should be nearly touching the ground, but keep it just an inch off the ground without letting it touch. Press yourself back up to the starting position by pushing with your front leg muscles, then jump up as high as you can and land softly on the ground in the same position you were in when you started. Step forward with your other leg, then repeat for 15 reps on each leg.

7. Burpees

This is another compound exercise that will get your heart pumping! Burpees are a full body exercise that burn a lot of calories and strengthen all of the major muscles in your body, including your arms, shoulders, back and chest. To do them, start standing up straight with feet shoulder-width apart and hands on hips or at shoulder height with palms facing down. Jump up as high as you can towards the ceiling by pushing from both legs and throwing both arms straight out in front of you. Press yourself back up to the starting position by bending at the knees and hips, then immediately jump into the air again and repeat for 15 reps.

8. Side Knee Lifts

This is another exercise that is great for toning your lower abdominal area! Start lying on a side with one leg straight out in front of you and the other bent at a 90 degree angle with foot flat on the ground. The bottom foot can be flat or you can lift it off of the ground slightly. Lift you top knee as high as you can towards your chest while keeping your hips up, then lower it back down to the starting position. Repeat for 50 reps, then switch sides and repeat with your other leg.

9. Mountain Climbers

This is another full body exercise that will get your heart pumping! Start out in a push-up position with back straight and feet together. With one leg, step forward so that your knee comes up to your chest while you are still in the push-up position. When you bring your knee back down to the floor, switch legs and repeat on that side. Repeat for 15 reps, then switch sides and repeat with your other leg.

10. Plank Jumps

This bodyweight exercise is an excellent workout for strengthening both of your arms since the resistance comes from holding yourself up! To do it, lie face down with upper torso off of the floor so that you are resting on forearms and toes. Hold yourself up as long as you can, then jump up and land softly on the floor. Repeat for 15 jumps.

11. Plank Holds

This exercise will help strengthen your core muscles and keep your body toned! To do it, lie face down on the floor with legs together and arms at your sides with palms facing down. Raise both legs off the ground as high as you can by bringing in both the front and back sides of both legs without dropping either of your shoulders or hips to the floor while holding yourself up with forearms and toes. Hold that position as long as you can, then lower yourself back to the starting position by slowly lowering both arms, feet and hips to the ground before repeating for 3 minutes.

Cardio Workouts are great because they get your heart rate up and help you stay focused during each exercise session. The key to success is to make sure you find a plan that will work for your body and your current fitness level. You should be able to push yourself each time you exercise, but you should also make sure that the exercises are challenging enough to allow room for progress when you return to that routine again. Only by pushing yourself will you see results, so find a workout plan that is right for you and start seeing changes today!

Cardio Workouts are great because they get your heart rate up and help you stay focused during each exercise session. The key to success is to make sure you find a plan that will work for your body and your current fitness level. You should be able to push yourself each time you exercise, but you should also make sure that the exercises are challenging enough to allow room for progress when you return to that routine again. Only by pushing yourself will you see results, so find a workout plan that is right for you and start seeing changes today!

This program is a perfect example of how getting in shape doesn't have to be hard or boring! If you currently don't have any workout routines, this plan has all of the tools and suggestions you need to get started on your path towards a healthier life.

Chapter 4: 15-Minute Training Plans

Cardio Workouts are great because they get your heart rate up and help you stay focused during each exercise session. The key to success is to make sure you find a plan that will work for your body and your current fitness level. You should be able to push yourself each time you exercise, but you should also make sure that the exercises are challenging enough to allow room for progress when you return to that routine again. Only by pushing yourself will you see results, so find a workout plan that is right for you and start seeing changes today! These 15-minute training plans can be used for aerobic workouts or resistance training. They are all great if you have little time in your day but want a quick, effective workout.

1. The 5-Minute Workout If you are really short on time and want to get an intense workout in, then this program is perfect for you. It's a great way to get your muscles pumping and to start sweating with just a few minutes of exercising!

2. The 10-Minute Workout This workout plan is easy and quick, yet still gets results! It can be used as a stand-alone workout plan or as extra cardio work after you have already performed a longer training session on another day. Many people find that it helps them lose weight and stay focused on exercise when they do this less intensive training after their long workouts are over for the week.

3. The 15-Minute Workout This full-body training program will get your heart pumping in just fifteen short minutes! It's a great way to get your body warmed up and ready for more intense workouts later in the week.

4. The 30-Minute Workout Many people find that they have time to exercise in the mornings before work, but if you have trouble keeping yourself motivated in the mornings, then this program is for you! This routine is designed to be done right after waking up so that it doesn't interfere with your breakfast or morning routine.

5. 30-Minute Upper Body Workout Whether you are trying to impress the ladies or just want to look good shirtless, this workout plan will give you the muscles you're looking for in just thirty minutes! This program is perfect for everyone - men, women and even children.

6. The 30-Minute Full Body Workout This full body training program is great for building muscle and increasing endurance. It's a perfect training plan to help you get into shape after a long break from working out or if you want to train more intensely than usual.

7. The 30-Minute Lower Body Workout If you want to really build muscle in your biceps, quads and calves, then this is the training plan for you. It's a great way to train all of the muscles in your lower body if you are trying to improve your overall strength or if you want to increase the muscle on a specific part of your body.

8. The 30-Minute Upper & Lower Body Workout This workout program is designed specifically for people who want to work on both their upper and lower body with equal intensity at the same time! It's a great training plan that will tone and strengthen your muscles while also working on mobility and endurance.

Full body program that uses both free weights and exercise machines to tone and strengthen your entire body. This workout plan is great for people who want to focus on building muscle or toning their entire body with just fifteen minutes of exercising each day. This training plan will get your heart pumping and help you burn fat all over your body! It's also great as a supplement to other training programs, so use it as an extra workout after you have already put in a longer training session. It's never too late to start becoming the best version of yourself!

This stand-alone workout plan is designed specifically for people who want to work on their upper body and nothing else. If you currently lift weights or do other exercises to build your muscles, then this workout plan can be added on after you have finished a longer training session that works on areas other than your arms, shoulders, chest and back. It's a great way to increase the intensity of your training sessions if you find yourself too tired or short on time for a longer workout later in the week. Use it alone or as an extra workout after you have completed a longer training routine on another day.

This bodyweight training program uses various muscles in your body to tone and strengthen your muscles. It's great for quick workouts that don't take too long but will still give you the results you are looking for! This program is also great for kids who want to keep their bodies healthy while they are growing up. This bodyweight training program is great for getting in shape without taking up your precious time! It's a great way to stay fit when you are travelling, working late or if you just have very little time for exercising. It will help keep your muscles strong and improve your endurance while helping you burn fat all over your body.

Endurance is essential for staying healthy and strong throughout the years. If you want to train your body to be able to run fast and far, then this program is perfect for you! It's designed to be a long distance training plan that will help you run faster and farther than ever before by increasing your endurance. It's perfect for people who already have experience running or prefer not to use weight training programs. This program will help you tone and strengthen your muscles while also building up the muscles in your legs. The best way to improve the strength of your legs is by increasing the amount of weight that they are lifting, so this program does just that!

This high intensity interval training (HIIT) workout plan is great for people who want a quick workout with high intensity. Your heart rate will be elevated for the entire workout plan, so this is a great way to burn fat and keep yourself in shape! It's also perfect for people who want to increase the intensity of their workouts but don't have much time to work out. Remember that you should only do this workout 2-3 times a week, as it is intense and will take its toll on your body if you do it more often.

Chapter 5: The Top 10 Motivators to Work Out for 15 Minutes or Less

Are you looking for some motivation to get your workout on? If you need a little extra push to get up and start exercising, then look no further. This chapter will provide you with the motivation and tools you need to get moving today! Motivation plays an important part in your ability to stay fit and healthy, so make sure that you have the proper motivation before heading out into the world for a run or a workout at the gym. This chapter will also give you some great tips on how to stay motivated when working out can be hard. These are all great ways that top athletes use to keep themselves motivated on days when they think they can't go on. When you're looking for a little motivation, remember that these athletes are regular people who use these techniques to push themselves harder. It may not work for everyone, but it's worth a shot! Here are the top ten motivators to get you started:

1. Exercise with Someone Who Keeps You Motivated Whether you are going to a class or working out alone at the gym, make sure you find someone who will keep you motivated throughout your workout. Working out with a friend can make workouts more enjoyable and will keep you pushing yourself until the very end.

2. Do Something You Love Sometimes exercising can be hard if it feels like a chore that doesn't make any sense to do in the first place. If you are looking for a way to make working out more fun, then try finding something you love to do that gets your heart racing. Maybe you like a certain sport, or maybe just jogging outside is what makes you happy. If there's something that makes your heart pump and your body move, then use it as a motivator to push yourself harder!

3. Set a Goal to Meet Sometimes it's easy to lose sight of why we're doing this in the first place. If you are looking for some motivation, then create a specific goal for yourself that will keep you on the right track towards success. If you want to lose weight, then keep that goal in mind every time you exercise and it will keep you focused on your success.

4. Plan a Specific Time for Working Out If you are looking for motivation, then the best way to stay motivated is to plan a specific time that you can work out. This is especially helpful if you have trouble staying motivated or getting up early in the morning. Even if it's just 5 minutes a day, planning specific times can help get your body moving even when you don't think you can.

5. Think About What You Could Do Without It Sometimes it's hard to understand what we have until we lose it altogether. If you are having trouble getting motivated, then think about what you would be missing if you weren't able to work out. What would your life be like if you hated going to the gym? Would your clothes fit right? Would your health be in danger? Would you look physically different with all of that extra weight on your body?

6. See Yourself at a Specific Weight When working out, sometimes it's easy to forget how far you have come and what your goal is in the first place. If you see a great picture of yourself looking fit and healthy, then use it as motivation to keep

going when things start getting tough. It will remind you of your original goal and keep you on the right track to success.

7. Listen to Motivating Music There are lots of ways to get motivated in the world today, and one of them is listening to music that makes you want to move! Music with a strong beat and energizing lyrics can really push you harder during your workout. Some people find it hard to get into a rhythm when exercising without music while others think it takes away from their workout, but no matter what, listening to specific songs can be great motivation when working out.

8. Focus on What You Have Already Achieved Working out is all about achieving as much as we possibly can. Sometimes it's easy to forget how far we have come with our workouts, but if you are having trouble getting motivated, then think about what you have already accomplished. Maybe you ran a mile this week or maybe your muscles look a little more toned. Think about everything that you have already done and use that as motivation to continue on the right track towards success.

9. Focus on What You Are Doing While Working Out Sometimes it can be hard to motivate yourself when working out because you don't feel like working out in the first place! If you are finding yourself lacking motivation, then try focusing on what your body is doing while exercising rather than focusing on actually doing the workout itself. This will help you stay focused and keep your motivation on the right track.

10. Use a Workout Buddy Having a workout buddy can be extremely helpful if you are looking for some extra motivation to get you through your workout plan. If you have someone to exercise with, then make sure that they are serious about their workouts so that they can push you harder! It may also help if they are trying

to do the same thing as you – whether that is losing weight or getting stronger – than working out with them will be a great way to reach your goal faster than ever before.

Chapter 6: The 15-Minute Workout Log

Keep track of your workouts with the workout log! This chapter will show you how to log your workouts for fifteen minutes or less. You will be able to keep track of your daily progress and create a custom workout plan that will keep you at a specific heart rate. This chapter will also give you some tips on how to make sure that your heart rate is right throughout each exercise. Depending on the workout program that you are using, it can be difficult to know exactly when to stop exercising during your training session. There are various ways to monitor this, but one of the best ways is using a heart rate monitor. It is most accurate if you have a heart rate monitor that works with your Smartphone, but it can also be used with free apps on your phone. This way, you can make sure that your heart stays in the right range and doesn't get too high or too low while working out. This is also great because it allows you to monitor your heart rate while running or exercising outside. If you plan on running, then make sure that your heart rate is monitored and stay in the correct heart rate zone. If you are looking for a quick way to monitor your heart rate, then you can always use a free app on your phone or hear rate monitor that is designed for high intensity workouts.

These are some of the best ways to keep track of your fitness:

1: The Basic Log This is probably one of the most common ways to track your workout. If you want something simple and easy to use, then this might be the best way for you. It's great because it's simple and it works! All you have to do is record basic information, such as the date and time, what you did during your workout, how long it took and maybe some additional notes about how it went. Record this in a notebook, on your computer or if you are using an app, then use that to log the information.

2: The Calorie Log If you are looking to lose weight, then this might be the log for you. This will help you keep track of your calories burned throughout the day and it will also tell you exactly how many calories you've burned during each workout session. This helps because it will keep track of everything for you and make sure that your fitness routine is working. It will also help to encourage you if things start getting tough because it will show how much progress you have made so far.

3: The Custom Log Depending on which fitness routine you are using, you might want to create a custom log. This way, you can keep track of everything that you should be doing and make sure that your body is getting what it needs. If there are certain exercises that you know your body needs, then make sure that those exercises are getting done! Use a spreadsheet or contact paper as a way to track your progress.

4: The Simple Log If you are looking for something simple and easy to use, then this might be the best choice for you. This will help keep track of some basic information and provide a little structure so that you know exactly how to keep track of your workouts. However, if you are using this log and you want more of a challenge, then try adding some extra exercises that you can do during your workout.

5: The Specific Log If you are looking for something simple and easy to use, but also want to keep track of your heart rate throughout the entire workout, then this might be the log for you. It has been designed specifically for workouts that last around fifteen minutes or less. All you have to do is follow the recommended heart rate zone that works best for your body and then record it throughout the workout. This way, you will know exactly what your heart rate should be at any given moment during the workout session.

6: The Workout Log Keeping track of your workouts is important whether you're training for a competition or just looking to get healthier and more fit. However, it can be a challenge to figure out what information you should be keeping track of and which information isn't necessary. This type of log will allow you to keep track of exactly how you are doing and how many calories you've burned during each workout session. It also keeps an accurate record of your heart rate zones so that you can make sure that your heart stays in the right range for the entire duration of the workout.

Chapter 7: The Equipment You Need

If you are going to be working out at home, then you will need a few pieces of equipment to really get the most out of your fitness routine. You don't have to have a lot of equipment in order to workout and be successful, but it would be ideal if you could find some good quality equipment that is easy for you to use. This chapter will show you the best types of equipment for using at home and how much each item costs.

The Best Equipment for Home Use

1: Two 5-pound dumbbells If you are just starting out and looking for something simple that won't cost much, then 5-pound dumbbells might be the right choice for you. These are usually the least expensive and can help you get in shape by using them for basic exercises. If you are looking for something to work your arms and shoulders, then these will be a great choice.

2: Two or Three 10-pound dumbbells If you are looking for something stronger than 5-pound weights, then 10-pound weights might be a better option for you. These will help build your strength and endurance much faster and are also good for working out your arms and shoulders.

3: One 25-pound dumbbell If you are looking to start lifting heavier weights, then this might be the best choice for you. This is also a good weight for working out your shoulders and arms.

4: A 10-pound medicine ball If you are looking to add some variety to your weight lifting routine, then a medicine ball will be a great choice for you. These are great for working out your upper body and building strength in your core. They can also help you improve balance and stability if you throw them around while working out.

5: A foam roller Foam rollers are a relatively new piece of equipment that have come about over the last few years of fitness training. If you have never tried one, then they can help relieve pain in your muscles after exercising or running long distances.

6: A weighted jump rope If you want to get a good jump rope, then this might be the best choice for you. These ropes come in various weights, but they are great for increasing your cardio and building up endurance. They are also really fun to use!

7: A jump mat This is another great choice and will help you stay safe while doing basic exercises like sit-ups or push-ups. These mats can also help decrease the risk of injury while doing cardio workouts.

8: Resistance bands If you need something to work your legs out without stepping on a treadmill or run outside, then resistance bands might be the right choice for you. These come in various sizes and are great for targeting specific muscles.

Finding the Best Equipment for Home Use If you are looking to purchase any of these items, then look online at stores like Target or Amazon, or try a local sports equipment store. Make sure that the equipment is high quality and will last you a long time. They should also be easy to use and should be able to help you reach your workout goals in no time!

Chapter 8: The Healthiest Foods on Earth: Super foods to Fuel Your 15-Minute Workouts and Other Health Longer.

This is a list of some of the healthiest foods on earth, as well as what they can do for you. These are great to have in your fridge, so make sure that you grab something healthy to eat after a hard workout session.

7 Food Superstars for Healthy Hearts Heart disease is one of the most common causes of death in America, but there are ways to keep your heart healthy. One of the best ways to do this is by eating healthy foods. These are the healthiest foods that you can eat for your heart and some of them may surprise you.

1: Grapefruit This crispy fruit is full of nutrients and vitamins that are good for your heart and blood vessels. They also have a lot of potassium in them, which helps lower blood pressure and reduce risk of stroke. If you're feeling like your heart isn't getting enough attention, then grapefruit might be a great way to help!

2: Avocados Remember these from your favourite guacamole? They actually have a ton of health benefits because they are filled with omega-3 fatty acids, vitamin E, vitamin C and potassium. They are also good for preventing coronary heart disease and cardiac arrest.

3: Oatmeal It might be common knowledge that oatmeal is good for your diet, but did you know that it is also great for your heart? It is full of soluble fibber which can help lower cholesterol and blood sugar levels.

4: Herring If you were looking to eat something savoury, then this might be what you're looking for! Herring has omega-3 fatty acids which help to reduce cholesterol and triglyceride levels in the blood. These are also great if you have a hard time eating leafy greens or other vegetables because they can be added to almost any dish.

5: Salmon Salmon is another fish that is great for your heart. It is full of omega-3 fatty acids and vitamin D, which are both important for reducing the risk of heart disease. This fish also has enough Omega-6 Omega-3 fatty acids to help your body absorb more fat and prevent heart disease and high blood pressure.

6: Tomatoes Remember to eat the skin because it may not be as healthy as you think! These bad boys are low in calories, but high in lycopene and antioxidants. They also have lots of fibre to help keep you full longer and improve digestion.

7: Beans These are one of those healthy foods that you probably remember from your childhood. They are great for heart health because they have lots of fibre, protein and potassium in them. If you don't like black beans, then you can try out some pinto beans or kidney beans as a way to help your heart stay healthy.

The Best Foods for Your Heart If you want to be sure that your heart is staying strong and healthy, then consider adding some of these foods to your diet. Eating healthy gives your body what it needs to stay healthy and also avoids some of the diseases that plague people every day.

The Best Foods for Your Brain

3 Super Foods for Focused Thinking and Improved Memory

If you want to keep your mind sharp and your memory intact, then you need to make sure that you are eating healthy foods. This focuses on three foods that are great for maintaining focus while exercising or just trying to get through work. These super foods also improve memory and can help keep your mind sharp while giving you a fun boost of energy when you need it most.

1: Walnuts This is a great source of omega-3 fatty acids and antioxidants that help to protect your brain from age-related memory loss. These nuts also contain lots of vitamin E, which is great for learning and memory.

2: Avocado Peppers This might be one of the most delicious super foods out there, but did you know that it is also full of good fats that can improve memory? It has vitamin B6 in it as well, which helps regulate blood sugar levels.

3: Wild Blueberries Blueberries are one of the healthiest fruits on earth and they come packed with nutrients that are good for your brain. These berries are also full of vitamin C, which helps to reduce stress and improve focus. If you eat a handful of these berries before a workout or before work, then you will be giving your body and mind the boost that it needs.

The Best Foods for Your Brain If you want to exercise your mind as well as your body, then consider eating any of these super foods on a regular basis. Those who eat healthy live longer and tend to have fewer health issues than those who don't!

The Best Foods for Your Colon

3 Super Foods for Happy Digestion

Your digestive system is responsible for absorbing nutrients from all the food in your diet. It needs to be healthy to get all the nutrients that you need, but it can also be affected by stress and illness. This will teach you about three foods that are great for improving digestion and keeping your colon in good shape!

1: Broccoli This might be a familiar vegetable, but did you know that it is great for your colon? It has lots of fibre, potassium and vitamin C in it, which are all essential in keeping your digestive system moving the right way.

2: Parsley Did you know that parsley is actually healthy? It is full of antioxidants and fibre that can help prevent bad stomach problems like constipation or diarrhoea. These are great for people who experience bloating or indigestion regularly.

3: Beans Beans are one of the healthiest foods on earth and they are full of fibre that will help clean out your colon. They also have lots of protein in them, which helps to regulate your stomach and improve digestion.

The Best Foods for Your Colon If you want to stay regular and happy, then consider eating any of these super foods on a regular basis. If you regularly have problems with bloating or indigestion, then this can help you regulate your stomach and get rid of the bloated feeling.

Chapter 9: The 15-Minute Mind-Body Workout Plan for a Better Brain and a Calmer You

This is a sample workout plan that can be used for working on your brain or body. You should be able to do this at home with very little equipment and it only takes 15 minutes! Just get yourself ready and go over the plan to see how you can work out your body in just 15 minutes. This is easier than you think!

1. 2-3 Warm Up Exercises This will help loosen up your muscles before you do the rest of the workout. Try walking for 3 minutes and then stretch your arms, legs, back and shoulders before you attack the rest of your workout.

2. 3-4 Strength Exercises These exercises will help build up your muscles and start to burn calories. Do each exercise for around 30 seconds and then take a short break before you move on to the next one.

3. 2-3 Cool Down Exercises If you are looking for something to cool down your body, then use the next few exercises to stretch out your muscles and get loose again. Try sitting down in a chair with your legs stretched out in front of you and lean back with one hand behind your head. This will help improve flexibility in your shoulders and hips.

4. 2-3 Stretching Exercises If you want to get even more flexible, then try three more stretches for your hips, legs and arms. Hold each stretch for around 30 seconds and then roll your shoulders and neck to loosen them.

5. 3-4 Breathing Exercises These breathing exercises are great for calming your mind and preparing you to finish the workout. They will also help regulate your heartbeat as well as boost energy levels. To do these exercises, breathing in through your nose for 3 counts and hold it in for 3 counts. Slowly exhale for 6 counts before taking a deep breath again.

6. 2-3 Deep Breathing Exercises You should also try out some deep breathing exercises at the end of the workout to help you relax. Breathing in through your nose for 5 counts and slowly exhale for 10 counts. Repeat this 6 times to get rid of stress and relax.

7. 2-3 Meditation Exercises If you want something a little more challenging, then meditation exercises are a great way to finish the workout. Sit down with your back straight, close your eyes and focus on your breathing for two minutes. This will help keep you relaxed and focused before continuing on with the rest of your day.

8. 2-3 Cool Down Exercises If you want to stretch out your muscles after the workout, then be sure to do it using the next few exercises. Try sitting in a chair with your legs outstretched in front of you and lean back with one hand behind your head. This will help improve flexibility in your hips and shoulders.

9. 3-4 Breathing Exercises You can also try out these breathing exercises at the end of the workout to help you relax further. Breathing in through your nose for 3

counts and hold it in for 3 counts. Slowly exhale through your mouth for 6 counts before taking a deep breath again.

Chapter 10: The 15-Minute Exercises You Can Do Anywhere

Did you know that you can do a workout without a gym? It's true! You can do it almost anywhere and with the right exercises, you can get in shape in less than 15 minutes. This is the best part of all because it doesn't matter where you are when your body needs to be exercised. Here are some of the best exercises that you can try out.

1. 2-3 Warm Up Exercises Warming up before your workout is one of the most important things that you need to do and it only takes about 5 minutes for this. You should start off by walking for 2 minutes and then stretch your arms, shoulders, legs and back for another minute. When you feel ready to move on, then you can jump right into the workout.

2. 3-4 Strength Exercises Pick 3 different exercises for your body and do each one for 1 minute before taking a break. You should try squats, lunges and pushups at first to work out your core as well as your legs. You can also try arm raises to work out your arms.

3. 3-4 Cool Down Exercises After you are done with the strength exercises, then use the next few minutes to cool down with some more stretching and

breathing exercises. Try sitting in a chair with your legs extended in front of you and lean back while resting one hand behind your head.

4. 2-3 Stretching Exercises After you have cooled down, then be sure to do some more stretching for your arms, legs and shoulders. You should also roll your neck and shoulders to loosen them up. If you want to take the best care of your body, then you should try out these exercises so that you can get back in shape in a safe and effective way!

5. 2-3 Breathing Exercises These exercises are great for relaxing your body and helping it to stay calm throughout the day. To do them, breathe in through your nose for 5 counts before holding it in for 10 counts. Slowly exhale through your mouth for 8 counts before taking another deep breath. This helps to reduce stress and calm your body down.

6. 2-3 Deep Breathing Exercises This is one of the hardest parts of any workout, but it's important that you try them out! To do these exercises, breath in through your nose for 5 counts and slowly exhale through your mouth for 10 counts. Repeat this 6 times to help relax your body and mind.

7. 2-3 Meditation Exercises These are the most difficult exercises of all because they take a lot of focus to do correctly. If you want something more challenging, then sit in a chair with your back straight, close your eyes and focus on breathing for 2 minutes. This will help keep you relaxed and focused whenever you need to be.

8. 3-4 Breathing Exercises You can also try out these breathing exercises at the end of your workout to help you relax. Breath in through your nose for 4 counts

and hold it in for 5 counts. Slowly exhale through your mouth for 8 counts before taking a deep breath again.

9. 2-3 Cool Down Exercises If you want to stretch out your muscles, then use the next few minutes to try some basic stretching exercises for your shoulders, arms and legs. This will help stretch out any tight muscles from the workout as well as loosen up tight joints that make it hard to move around easily.

10. 2-3 Stretching Exercises If you want to do a little more, then try some more stretching exercises for your arms, legs and shoulders. You should also roll your neck and shoulders to loosen them up and improve flexibility.

Chapter 11: A New You in Just 15 Minutes.

If you follow the workout plan in this book and eat healthy, then you will start to see a difference in your body and health. Your body will be happier, stronger and more flexible than ever before. This is how:

Eating Healthy You might have heard that eating healthy is the best way to improve your health, but do you know how it works? The food that we put into our bodies has to be able to digest easily so that we can absorb all of the nutrients that we need. If the food does not digest well, then it will go through your colon and get trapped there for a long time. This will cause your colon to become sluggish and fat deposits will build up behind the stool. Over time, your colon will get bigger and bigger because your body is not getting the nutrients that it needs. Your digestive system will eventually get blocked because it can no longer push the stool through your colon and out of your body. If you constantly eat foods that are hard to digest, then you will have to deal with serious lifestyle issues in the future. This is why you need to change your diet and start eating more vegetables and fruits instead of processed foods. You will also want to stop drinking soda or alcohol if you currently do. These drinks are full of sugar, which is hard for your body to absorb if you don't have enough fibre in your diet. Your digestive system needs fibres so that it can get rid of the unabsorbed food. If you are trying to lose weight, then focus on eating more vegetables and fruits. This will help you to get rid of excess water and boost your metabolism at the same time. You should also avoid fried foods because they are high in fat as well as saturated fats that will stick to the walls of your colon. You need to avoid this because it will make your body start to swell up and cause digestive problems like constipation, bloating or diarrhoea. Fiber is also very important for keeping a healthy digestive system and you can get it by eating lots of green leafy vegetables, oatmeal, oat bran, wheat bran and whole grains. Over time, you will see a huge difference in your digestive health and you should start to have much less constipation and bloating. Your body will no longer hold onto excess water or get impacted by extra pounds. You can also add some probiotic yogurt into your diet because it contains good bacteria that helps break down food so that it can be digested. This is very helpful for those that have digestive issues like diarrhoea because the good bacteria restores balance to their intestines after being sick or drinking certain beverages.

3-4 Minutes of Exercise Doing a few minutes of exercise every day will improve the way that your body moves. You will start to feel stronger, more flexible and much more relaxed. In fact, it only takes around 3 minutes of exercise to realize some of the health benefits which is why you should add 15 minutes into your busy schedule every day. Since you can do this in your own home or office, there are no excuses not to do it! When it comes to moving your body around, then try out some squats with weights and lunges. You should also try going for a walk around the block or even running up and down flights of stairs if you have the time. If you want to get even more movement in your body, then you should try out some yoga poses every day. You can do the sun salutation stretch or do some of the simpler moves like downward facing dog or child's pose.

3-4 Minutes of Breathing Exercises It is also important that you take the time to focus on breathing exercises that will help you to calm down and relax. You should try three different breathing exercises every day for at least 3 minutes each. Try out the diaphragmatic breath, corpse pose and box breathing exercise so that you can clear your mind and relax your body.

3-4 Minutes of Deep Breathing Exercises The most important thing that you can do is to practice deep breathing every day for a few minutes. This will help you to relax and calm down when you are feeling stressed or anxious. You should practice breathing exercises by sitting in a chair with your back straight and then breathe in through your nose for 5 counts before slowly exhaling through your mouth for 10 counts. Repeat this 6 times so that you can start to clear your mind and relax.

2-3 Minutes of Meditation Exercises If you want something that is a little more challenging, then focus on practicing meditation exercises every day for 2 to 3 minutes. This will help you to feel happy and relaxed for the rest of your day. You should sit somewhere comfortable with your back straight before closing your eyes and focusing on breathing for 2 minutes. This is a great way to get in a relaxed state and focus on the good things in your life as well as forget about everything else!

The Benefits Of Working Out In A Group

If you are trying to lose weight or get into shape, then you might be wondering whether it's better to do these things alone or with a group of friends. In fact, you can do both because each method has its own advantages and disadvantages. Here are some reasons as to why you might want to join a group in the future.

3-4 Reasons To Work Out In A Group

1. Accountability When you work out in a group, then it is easy to get distracted or start talking about other things that are going on in your life. This is why it's important for everyone to hold each other accountable so that they can be sure that the workout will happen as planned and nothing else will come up. When everyone is working out together, then no one wants to let the other people down by not being there or doing exercises incorrectly.

2. Motivation If you are suffering from motivation issues, then you should join a group so that you can enjoy the fun of working out with your friends.

3. Healthy Competition Working out in a group will also help you to have healthy competition to keep your body motivated and moving in the right way. You should always expect to get the best results if you are working out with other people because this will encourage everyone to stay on track. It's important for everyone to keep each other accountable so that everyone succeeds together and it's not just one person that gets healthier while others go back to eating unhealthy foods or giving up on their goals.

4 Things To Do When Joining A Group

a. Try Out Different Workout Classes There are so many workout classes available for you to choose from, so it can be hard to know where to start. Luckily, you can try out different classes until you find one that matches your fitness level and goals. You should try out a class that is something new to you every few weeks so that you get the most benefits possible.

b. Check Your Level Of Skill If the rules of the class are too hard for you, then talk to your instructor about working at a different skill level or coming back again when your skills have improved. It's a terrible feeling to attend a high-level class when you are not ready to do the exercises yet, so talk to the instructor if you have any skill or ability issues.

c. Get To Know The Skill Of Other People One of the most important things that you can do is work out with other people that are at your skill level so that you can encourage each other to stay motivated and get better results over time. You should also talk to the others about what they like most about working out in a group and how they enjoy motivating each other on social media.

d. Workout With Other People For Accountability Having someone to work out with for accountability is very important and you should definitely invite your friends to join you as well. If they already work out, then it will be easy to go at the same time and do the same exercises. You can even take turns encouraging each other as you workout so that no one gets distracted by their surroundings or weakens when they are having a bad time.

3-4 Things To Avoid When Working Out in a Group
1. Obsessing Over Weight If you are truly working out with other people for motivation, then you should know that they are focused on their own results more than yours. If they want to lose weight, then they will follow their own program and it might be different from your workout plan so don't let this bother you. You can check out the same workout plan that your friend is following so that you push each other to stay accountable.

2. Spreading Bad Energy If you can't help but be negative about your workout or results, then don't bother joining a group. You will only end up spreading bad energy to others and they will lose faith in their fitness program.

3. Not Staying Safe If you are trying to work out in a group, then it's important to make sure that everyone is staying safe at all times throughout the exercises so

that no one gets injured. If you see that someone is doing something wrong, then point it out and see if they can correct their form so that they don't get hurt.

4. Not Getting Results You should also be aware that it might be a little harder to get results when you are working out in a group because you aren't sure what might affect your results. It's important for everyone to follow the same workout schedule so that everyone gets the results that they want over time.

The Benefits Of Yoga In a Mat

Yoga in a mat is a great exercise to try out because it will help you to have more flexibility, a stronger core and better balance. You should add this exercise to your workout schedule if you are looking for something new and low impact so that you can get the best results possible. To do this, follow these instructions.

1. Sitting Position The first step is to sit down on a soft mat with your legs crossed and your hands in your lap. You want to either have the palms facing up or the fingers pointing toward the top of your head before you begin breathing exercises.

2. Breathing Exercises Next, you need to focus on your breathing by doing a breathing exercise for 3-4 minutes. You should breathe in for 5 counts before exhaling for 10 counts. You can practice this note breathing exercise for about 6 times to start feeling more relaxed and calm.

3. Lying Position Next, you need to lie down on your back before taking the time to focus on your breathing for 2 minutes. You should close your eyes and focus on breathing in for 5 counts before breathing out for 10 counts. This is a great way to get in a relaxed state and think about the things that are making you happy.

4. Sitting Position You can sit up after a few minutes and take the time to repeat the process once again if you want something more challenging or if you feel like being active.

5. Balancing Pose The next step is to stand up while you are holding a balancing pose for at least 3 minutes. You can do the tree pose, half moon, or warrior 1 pose to get in better shape and have a stronger core. You will feel much more flexible when you are done with this exercise and you should focus on getting a good stretch in your legs and back.

6. Standing Position Next, you should stand up while focusing on moving your body for another 2 minutes. While holding this position, you want to move around as much as possible so that you start burning fat from different areas of your body.

Conclusion

There are so many great exercises that you can do when working out in a group that can have an amazing impact on your life. You should definitely try these out because they are all exercises that someone else has already done and loved. If you want to get the best results possible, then focus on eating a healthy diet and exercising consistently. If you want extra motivation, then join a group and get better goals with friends! It's important for everyone to move their body and create new habits every day so that they can get healthier over time.

There are so many fun and interesting exercises that you can do when working out in a group, so it's important for everyone to try these out today. Who knows, you might even get the best results possible because of the people around you! It is also important to practice deep breathing every day for a few minutes so that you can calm down and relax your body when you are feeling anxious. This might be the most crucial part of working out in a group because it will get easier as time goes on. If you start focusing on your breathing every day, then it will only get easier for everyone who is living life with anxiety.